KV-392-173

Contents

For Nev, Rose & Barnaby

Foreword

Over the last few years I have become fascinated by the subject of addiction and, in particular, the search for new ways to help smokers escape from a most distressing and damaging drug dependence. 'Hard' drugs that can kill quickly, like heroin, are viewed with fear and alarm by society at large even though they kill a relatively small number of people. Tobacco, on the other hand, kills slowly but surely and is responsible for the untimely, lingering deaths of countless millions around the world. According to current UK death rates, for every 1000 young adults who smoke regularly: 1 will be murdered, 6 will die in road accidents but a staggering 500 (50%) will die because of their tobacco use. Smoking is all the more powerful and insidious because it can work its way into every aspect of a person's life and even seems to enter the personality, persuading the individual that without tobacco they will be somehow diminished. The reverse is true, however, for when people successfully escape from 'the smoking trap' they usually feel a great sense of achievement and gain more control over their lives as a result.

The World Health Organisation (WHO) has warned that we face a huge global increase in suffering and premature death from cancer, heart disease and other lifestyle-related illnesses in the next 25 years. If current smoking patterns continue, the numbers killed by tobacco each year will rise from about 3 million in 1990 to 10 million in 2030. As people in the Western, developed world realise that smoking is dangerous and smoking rates decline, the tobacco companies are actively targeting other populations, where awareness of the risk is low and potential profits are high. It is, therefore, enormously important that we share our knowledge of this subject with those whose children are at increasing risk from the greed of the tobacco companies.

Stopping smoking works! Giving up at any time will prolong life, improve the quality of that life and reduce the risks of developing a range of tobacco-related illnesses such as cancer and heart disease. Stopping when you are young or in middle-age (35-69) is especially beneficial but stopping at any age is a good idea. After several decades of expensive research into what it takes to stop successfully we do now know which strategies work best and new and better treatments are being developed all the time. I firmly believe that stopping successfully is a skill, and, as such, it can be learned. It is not a magic process or a talent restricted to the lucky few. Mastering this skill takes time, application and a willingness to analyse feelings and situations. A degree of determination is certainly part of what's required but it's not 'rocket science' and I've seen people from all walks of life succeed. It may take a few attempts to get it right but you learn as you go along, and with continued effort you can win through in the end.

I have enjoyed working with many individual smokers and have also been lucky to learn from a number of knowledgeable colleagues and researchers, without whose help and contributions the writing of this book would not have been possible. These are: Professor Robert West, Dr Jonathan Foulds, Dr Peter Hajek, Dr Chris Steele, Gay Sutherland, Charlie Manicom, Andy McEwen, Sylvia May, Gabrielle Harris, Cathy Myles and Chris Blunkell.

Introduction

The STOP! Guide to Stopping Smoking

Giving up smoking successfully and permanently is not only possible but a bloody good idea to boot! Thousands of people are living happier, healthier and wealthier lives as a result of breaking their addiction to tobacco and there is absolutely no reason why you shouldn't be one of them. There is no magic involved in stopping for good and those who manage it are not super-humans with barrow-loads of willpower to spare. On the contrary, they are ordinary people who came to the conclusion that they didn't want tobacco to dominate their lives and ruin their health. What distinguishes them from those who are still trying to stop is perhaps that they used the right treatments and self-help strategies to help them do the job and they used them effectively. This book will arm you with all the tools and information you need. It is not a 'miracle programme' or some kind of spiritual aid, it is rather a practical guide to the skill of breaking your addiction to tobacco smoking and changing your daily behaviour. Once you've mastered this skill you will be able to stop smoking completely and enjoy your new smoke-free life to the full. You may also find that having beaten tobacco addiction, you go up in your own esteem and feel ready to tackle other challenges and achieve more in life as a result.

PUZZLING IT OUT

Quitting successfully is a bit like doing a jigsaw puzzle in that you can't get it right if you don't have all the pieces. In this case the 'pieces' are things like: products to help you get through the first few days, distraction tactics to help occupy your mind and emergency strategies for sudden cravings. If you only have a few of these 'pieces' then you might get through the first day, only to relapse later when a friend offers you a cigarette. Alternatively, you might crack up after just a couple of hours because you were bored, angry or sad and had no remedies to hand.

WE HAVE THE TECHNOLOGY!

Thirty years of research into what it takes to quit successfully have taught scientists and psychologists a great deal about the best ways to escape from tobacco addiction and it's time to pass that information on to those who need it most. There is no single thing that will make it all effortless and you will need to use your imagination and ingenuity to win through. There are, however, many effective products and proven strategies that you can use to help you and it needn't be nearly as difficult as your addicted mind would have you believe. Parts of the process may even be enjoyable (yes, I did say 'enjoyable'!). You'll need to use different tactics to combat the physical and the psychological aspects of the addiction and other skills to avoid relapsing later but you don't need to be Einstein to master it. Planning and anticipating possible problems is half the battle and as in other areas of life, practice makes perfect! I've already said that giving up is like putting a jigsaw puzzle together. It could just as well be said that there is a recipe for success and you need to have all the ingredients if you want the finished product to turn out right. This book contains all the ingredients and if you read it carefully you will be equipped for the job of stopping for good. The rest will then be up to you.

And Who The Hell Am I?

Given that this is an important subject and one that could change your life, you have every right to know who I am, and why I think I'm qualified to tell you how to give up smoking. My credentials to write on this subject are as follows. Firstly, I am an ex-smoker. My personal experiences in battling the weed aren't necessarily all that relevant to yours, as people vary, but in your shoes I'd want to know if this book had been written by an ex-smoker or a 'never-smoker'. The facts are that I smoked at least 25 to 30 cigarettes every day from the age of sixteen to the age of thirty-one when I finally managed to stop (following numerous botched attempts). During my smoking years I truly felt that being a smoker was part of my personality and that non-smokers were somehow 'less interesting' as people. I loved my cigarettes with a passion and believed that smoking was one of life's great pleasures. I am also a coward, however, and as time went by I became more and more afraid of what I might be doing to myself, and then later, to my family.

In 1990 I started working with people who were struggling to overcome a variety of addictions to substances like cocaine, heroin and alcohol. I learned more about the physical and mental processes of addiction and decided that if others could change their lives for the better then so could I. My motivation to quit was strong and previous failed attempts to stop had taught me quite a lot about what *not* to do! I suppose that by then I had enough of the pieces of the puzzle to make it work and I managed to do it at last. I was surprised by how much easier it was to succeed. After only 3 days things got a lot better and I realised that all my failed attempts had been much more agonising than actually allowing myself to move forward and progress through the crucial first few days.

THE BENEFIT OF HINDSIGHT

Since stopping I have realised that my 'love' of smoking was entirely created by my addiction to tobacco and that, as an addict, my thoughts were heavily influenced by my need to know where my next cigarette was coming from. It's only by looking back, some time after quitting, that the scale of the smoking 'con trick' and the power of tobacco addiction can fully be appreciated and that's why many current smokers find it impossible to imagine that life without tobacco can be worthwhile or enjoyable. Your head seems to know that that doesn't make sense, but fear and addiction make your heart feel very differently. A great many quit attempts fail before they ever start because almost as soon as the smoker thinks 'maybe I should stop', their addiction pipes up with, 'of course you can't' or, 'life will be no fun if you do'. So, if you'd like to stop smoking don't worry if these negative thoughts pop into your head. They're part of the addiction and other people get them too. Try to ignore them for the time being and remember that your desire to quit is based on good logic. If you follow the programme in this book then you won't actually stop smoking until you've done some serious planning and gathered together a whole bunch of things to help you so there's really no need to panic.

THERE'S NEVER BEEN A BETTER TIME TO STOP!

For the last few years I have specialised in research into stopping smoking and I've been fortunate to work alongside some of the best-known and most talented researchers in the UK. With their help, I have counselled hundreds of would-be stoppers in a number of research trials and clinics. New and better treatments for smokers are constantly being developed around the world and in many ways there's never been a better time to quit. The key is to give people the information they need to put it all together and help themselves. In order to do this I set up STOP! Magazine in 1998. STOP! is a fun, colourful, self-help magazine for smokers and it combines motivational success stories with information about the best quitting techniques. It's a kind of ongoing support package for people who are thinking about stopping or who are actually in the process of doing so. This book takes a similar, practical approach and could be used on its own or with the magazine. It covers all aspects of stopping so that you can find the best combination of strategies for you. There are some good 'stop smoking' books about, but many focus on one specific programme or technique and sometimes ignore rival therapies. The STOP! Plan provides advice on a wide range of approaches and treatments as well as a clear, step-by-step programme to help you negotiate the obstacles that may lie ahead. Use it, learn from it and move on, just as you would in other areas of your life. Giving up smoking is an important (life-saving) task that needs to be tackled urgently but you don't want to be doing it over and over again for years to come! Get the facts and then get it over with so that you can enjoy all that life has to offer for as long as possible.

GET IN TOUCH

If you want to tell others about your 'stopping' experiences or comment on this book then do please write to us at the address on the fly-leaf. Your progress might make a great success story for STOP! Magazine and your favourite strategies could help someone else to succeed – so get reading and good luck!

CHAPTER 1

Myths and Misconceptions

Tobacco has been around for a long time, and scientists have known that smoking is bad for you for a good 30 or 40 years. Unfortunately, despite all the research and the health information that governments and health agencies have put out, a great many smokers are still ignorant about some very basic tobacco-related facts. We'll start by getting these straight, and then you'll be better equipped to learn about stopping successfully.

1. THE 'SMOKING HELPS WITH STRESS' MYTH

The idea that you need tobacco to help you cope with the stresses and strains of everyday life is one of the strongest and most widely believed smoking myths. The physical side of nicotine addiction helps to reinforce it for reasons we'll go into in a minute, but the plain fact of the matter is that smoking does *not* relieve stress! You were born able to cope with stressful events and situations and once you've stopped smoking for good you'll be calmer and better able to cope with whatever life throws at you. Smokers actually have *higher* baseline stress levels than non-smokers or ex-smokers who have passed through the early 'withdrawal phase' of quitting and this can be measured reliably in scientific studies.

Q. So why does it feel like smoking reduces stress?
Regular smokers are used to having a certain level of nicotine
in their bodies. You get some nicotine whizzing up to your
brain every time you take a puff on a cigarette, cigar or pipe.
This usually takes about 4 seconds, but the drug leaves your
brain almost as quickly, so it doesn't take very long (about 20
minutes for most regular smokers) for your body to start missing it and wanting another 'hit'. If you can't get any more nicotine for some reason then you'll start to experience the
symptoms of nicotine withdrawal (agitation, irritation and a
strong desire to smoke) and your stress levels rise as a result.
The next time you smoke, the nicotine quickly relieves the
withdrawal symptoms and so your stress levels fall and you
feel better almost immediately. This chain of events happens
umpteen times every day to most smokers, although they may
not really be aware of it unless they are deprived of a smoke for
a long time. Over the years the impression that whatever
you're doing, you feel better and less stressed with a cigarette,
gets firmly implanted in your mind and it's a hard belief to shift
when you've smoked for a long time. For the moment you'll
need to take that information on trust but when you've stopped
smoking and passed through the withdrawal phase, you'll feel
much calmer and then it'll seem much more believable.

Q. How does smoking increase stress levels?
Cigarette smoke has a stimulant effect on your body, it
increases your blood pressure and your heart rate and locks
you into a cycle of withdrawal and relief that is itself stressful.
You've probably experienced those 'Oh no, I'm running out of
cigarettes' moments, just like most other smokers, and the
constant need to be thinking about where your next cigarette
is coming from and when you'll next be able to smoke. This
need to keep smoking in itself adds a stressful element to
what may already be a busy and challenging life. Hardened
tobacco addicts will walk two miles in the rain to get cigarettes

from a late-night garage if they're worried about running out and even less dependent smokers keep a 'weather' eye on the number of cigarettes left in their packets. If you're also going through a particularly tricky life-event, or relationship problems at the time then your stress levels could rocket, you may think that you can't possibly cope without a smoke to steady your nerves. Precisely the reverse is true. When you do quit your pulse rate will probably drop by about 8 beats per minute and you won't give two hoots about where the nearest tobacconist's shop or vending machine is and that really will be relaxing!

*Leaving a warm home to find a cigarette machine
when you are desperate can be a bit of a bind*

2. THE 'LIFE WON'T BE ANY FUN WITHOUT SMOKING' MYTH

The idea that smoking is one of life's great pleasures and that without it, life will be a drab, meaningless existence devoid of any real enjoyment is common amongst addicted smokers. It is also completely false and is often used as a reason for relapsing in the early stages of a quit attempt or for not bothering to try to stop at all. You only have to look at non-smokers or long-term ex-smokers to see that they're just as happy, sad, mad or bad as the rest of us. They're not a bunch of scaredy-cat introverts who didn't have the bottle to sample life properly and they don't walk the streets in a constant state of terminal depression either! The pleasure associated with smoking is almost completely derived from the fact that it relieves tension and withdrawal symptoms in the short-term. Fear of the unknown and anxiety about doing without cigarettes are quite natural and understandable when you're thinking about stopping for good and this myth may creep into your mind before you can make the break from tobacco. Recognise it for what it is (illogical claptrap!) and you won't be derailed before you've even got started.

3. THE 'UNCLE BILLY/AUNT MABEL' MYTH

Another argument that often comes up when people are deciding whether it's really worth stopping smoking is the one about good old Uncle Billy/Aunt Mabel. These indomitable characters, we are told, smoked 60 a day from the age of ten, drank a bottle of whisky every night and still lived to the ripe old age of ninety-three without suffering a moment's ill health! It's amazing how many people seem to have met these hardy souls, and a few of them must exist somewhere. But sadly the truth of the matter is that for every Uncle Billy or Aunt Mabel, there are thousands more life-long smokers who die younger, sicker and sadder as a result of their addiction. There really isn't any doubt on this one so I don't propose to labour the point in this book, or go into graphic detail about the ghastly effects of smoking on the body. Just don't let those anecdotes about exceptional cases fool you into thinking that you'll probably be lucky and escape the effects of smoking because the odds really aren't in your favour. As the comedian Dave Allen said in the course of an interview about why he stopped for good, 'Smoking is like playing Russian roulette with six bullets in the chamber, it will kill you if you don't stop.'

4. THE 'YOU MIGHT GET HIT BY A BUS ANYWAY' MYTH

This is a great oldchestnut which I'm sure you'll have heard before if you haven't actually said it yourself, and of course it's absolutely true, you could get hit by a bus tomorrow and some people will, although I must admit that I've never actually met anyone who did. The thing to remember here, is that most of us try to look both ways when we cross the road and so, for the most part, avoid getting involved in traffic accidents. We also avoid falling down manholes and refrain from swallowing householdbleach alongwith other activities that are likely to do us harm. Carrying on smoking for years and years is more like hurling yourself in front ofbuses on a regular basis and putting bleach in your tea every weekend! You might get away with it a few times but in the long-term your prospects aren't good.

5. THE 'YOU NEED LOADS OF WILLPOWER TO QUIT AND I HAVEN'T GOT ANY' MYTH

It is a sad fact that a great many, otherwise confident, talented people remain convinced that it's only possible to give up smoking if you're born with large amounts of that most desirable commodity 'willpower'. Memories of past failed attempts and the scepticism of friends and family when you announce 'I'm really going to quit this time' seem to eat away at the self-esteem of many stoppers and unfortunately ex-smokers sometimes make matters worse by claiming to have stopped without much effort 'just like that!'. This would seem to indicate that they merely had to turn on the old 'willpower tap' and then they were 'home and hosed'. The reality for most stoppers is that they are unsure and anxious to start with, but with every day they manage not to smoke, their confidence and self-esteem go up a notch. There are tricky times of course, when they need to use a variety of strategies to stay on track (more on these later) but for the most part 'willpower' seems to grow with your progress, day by day. Once people

have put smoking behind them they often feel more confident to tackle other challenges and the skills they've mastered in changing their smoking behaviour can come in handy in a whole host of other situations in life that require perseverance and forward planning. (Refer to the section on Willpower in Chapter 5 for more on how to make the most of your willpower.)

CHAPTER 2

Getting Motivated

Do You Really Want to Stop?

This might sound like a silly question, as the simple fact that you're reading this book suggests that you're already fairly keen to have a bash at stopping, but most people find that their level of motivation waxes and wanes from day to day. It depends on their mood and the situation they find themselves in. On certain days when, for example, your smoker's cough is playing you up, or you've just noticed that your fingers are turning yellow, you may feel very strongly that you want to escape from tobacco addiction and you may decide to make a real effort to stop. At other times, however, such as when you're out with friends or as the Quit Day draws ominously close, things may be different. You may feel that the time just isn't right and that it's too much to expect of yourself on top of everything else that's going on in your life. This 'Jekyll and Hyde' switching between opposing points of view is pretty common with smokers who want to stop and it echoes the struggle going on in their heads. On the one hand, their reason tells them that quitting is indeed the best plan, but when push comes to shove and actual abstinence looms on the near horizon, the frightened, addicted child inside them searches for any and every reason to put it off or find reasons to avoid stopping altogether. At this point all the myths that we've just 'debunked' will probably come tumbling out as the smoker mentally digs their heels in and reaches for their cigarette packet. Don't worry if your thinking veers from positive to negative in this way, it doesn't mean that you're cracking up or that you don't have any willpower. It happens to most smokers when they consider quitting and if you learn to recognise negative thinking as part of your psychological addiction then at least you won't doubt your sanity!

PUTTING IT OFF

I well remember telling people quite confidently and reasonably that I would give up when I was more 'settled'. I'm not quite sure what I meant by this, but as the years crept by I began to realise that the time was never going to feel totally right for stopping and that 'settled' could end up meaning 'six feet under' if I didn't get on with it. Another favourite self-deception trick of mine was to boldly announce that I was going to quit and then to have a half-hearted go at stopping (which was doomed to failure for a variety of reasons). When, after a few hours of thoroughly martyred abstinence, I'd relapsed and was safely back with my cigarettes in my hand, I'd award myself a nice 6 to 12 months of 'guilt-free smoking'. 'After all', I'd tell myself, 'I had a go and I'll try again some day when the time is right or the wind is in the right direction, or my life is stress-free etc. etc.'

GRASP THAT NETTLE
(BEFORE IT STINGS YOU!)

My experiences may not all be relevant to you as each one of us is different but if this kind of thinking has ever delayed your escape from the weed then maybe it's time to stop giving yourself the run-around and face facts. Stopping is a job that needs doing and it won't go away until you do it. There are more interesting things to do with your life than worry about when and how to quit smoking so why not get it out of the way sooner rather than later? If you approach it systematically and prepare well then you need never do it again – and preparing well is what this book is all about. Use it to prepare your mind, your body and your surroundings and you will be ready and able to take action.

Your Smoking (and Stopping) Career

Some lucky people manage to stop for good at their first attempt but most of us try and fail a few times before we crack it (on average about 7 times). A typical smoker's career goes through some fairly predictable stages and the desire to escape from tobacco addiction builds slowly the older you get. See if you recognise your past or present smoking attitudes from the examples here.

THE HAPPY SMOKER

Smokers in their teens or early twenties don't worry too much about their tobacco use:

> *'I'm young and healthy so why should I worry?'*

THE SLIGHTLY CONCERNED
PARENT/TWENTY-SOMETHING

As time goes by, slightly older smokers start to consider the merits of stopping more seriously:

> *'I can't afford to smoke now and I worry about the children's health'*

THE SERIOUSLY WORRIED SMOKER

By the time most smokers reach their thirties and forties the signs of smoking-related disease have begun to show and their worries multiply:

'I can't run upstairs without getting out of breath and I'm always getting colds on my chest'

The Stages of Change

A few years ago, two psychologists from the US (James Prochaska and Carlo Di Clemente) came up with a model of the stages that smokers often go through on their way to quitting smoking for good. This was called the 'Stages of Change' model and it became very popular as a means of describing the 'process' smokers seem to go through. According to the theory, giving up smoking is a rather cyclical (circular) process. Smokers move from being in PRECONTEMPLATION (the 'happy smoker' we've just described) to CONTEMPLATION (the 'concerned' smoker) and from there to the ACTION stage, in which they actually try to quit. After a quit attempt, things may go one of two ways. Either the person succeeds in staying off cigarettes and 'escapes', or they relapse and go back around the cycle again, maybe moving through the stages a bit quicker this time. When I first learned about this model it made a certain amount of sense to me because, looking back, I remembered going through a similar process many times before I eventually quit. In fact, towards the end of my smoking 'career' I felt as if I was going around it so often it was like being in a washing machine on the spin cycle! If this rings any bells with you then take heart, because previous trips around the cycle may have helped to prepare you to get it right next time. Trying to stop smoking is never a waste of time and the effort you have invested up to now will stand you in good stead later on when we come to analyse the causes and prevention of relapse. For now, though, your task is to build your motivation and get ready to succeed.

Real Success Stories

Thousands of people the world over have escaped from tobacco and are living examples that it can be done. We've featured many of their stories in STOP! Magazine and as well as being happier and healthier as a result of stopping, they all express a desire to help others escape and enjoy the same benefits. When you're still smoking it's all too easy to dismiss ex-smokers as weirdos with no social life to speak of, or evangelical bigots with an axe to grind about those who still smoke, but this is just another example of distorted, addiction-type thinking. When a person manages to break their physical and psychological addiction to tobacco the effects are pretty dramatic and I'm not just talking about their physical health. Most ex-smokers enjoy a new-found sense of self-esteem, they really start liking and believing in themselves again because they've stopped running away from a problem and tackled it successfully. After years and years of evasion and excuses they are at last free to get on with their lives and can truly relax without the need to fire stimulants into their brains umpteen times a day. Looking back it's often hard for ex-smokers to comprehend how they could have allowed themselves to remain in the tobacco trap for so long and, quite naturally they want to help others to escape from it too.

Here are a few quotes from some of the successful ex-smokers we've featured in STOP! Magazine:

' I regard giving up smoking as an enormous achievement. I realised that I could take control over other aspects of my life and that I was finally free. The main benefits are the self-confidence, the self-esteem and the amazing freedom!'

ANNE ROBINSON

'I really enjoy my life as a non-smoker and if anyone offers me a cigarette I enjoy saying, "No, thanks, I don't."'

MARISA PARDUCCI

'I consider giving up smoking to be a key achievement in my life. It has shown me that I can do difficult things if I try. If there is something about the way I am that doesn't please me, I can change it. It might sound obvious, but I haven't always felt that way.'

CHRIS BLUNKELL

'If anyone out there is thinking of quitting I'd say go for it! Believe in yourself and you really can do it.'

LINDA HEYES

'Once your mind's made up you really can give up smoking. Don't betray yourself and don't let those silly excuses make you break your word. Just try it and it'll get easier and easier with every day that passes.'

DAVE ALLEN

HOLIER THAN THOU?

Ex-smokers may genuinely want to help their smoking friends and relatives to enjoy the same benefits that they've discovered so they often try to persuade them to quit but this is where things can go wrong, especially if they come on a bit too strong or focus on the 'smoking is smelly' aspect too much. Ex-smokers usually regain their sense of smell quite wonderfully within a few weeks of quitting and are quite shocked when they realise how strongly they must have smelled of tobacco in the past but it's not very tactful to emphasise this aspect to current smokers who may feel personally insulted and dismiss everything else said to them. It can also be counter-

productive if ex-smokers announce that quitting is really easy
and that they stopped 'just like that'. Some people do say this
and it's guaranteed to get your back up if you're still trying to
find your way out of the smoking 'maze'. It implies that there's
nothing to it and that you're a bit of a 'mug' because you
haven't cracked it yet. It's also very likely that the smoker in
question actually tried to quit a few times before succeeding
and went through various mental stages before being able to
make the break successfully. Motivation usually builds up in a
smoker over the years and stopping is rarely the result of some
kind of overnight 'conversion'. The message here is really
don't let tactless ex-smokers put you off, they may be a bit
'OTT' or seem to be nagging when they urge you to stop but
that's just because they want to help and don't really know
how to get their message over. Get ready to stop at your own
pace and get motivational 'ammunition' from the positive
aspects of what ex-smokers have to say. A good understanding
of the benefits will help you later on and you'll soon develop a
personal sense of what success can bring. Stopping isn't a com-
petition sport; it's not important who gave up first or how
quickly, all that really matters is that you manage to do it successfully in your own time.

12 Reasons to Stop For the New Millennium (and Yourself!)

1. More Money!
You may never win the lottery but if you give up smoking
your disposable income is sure to increase. There are oodles
of nice things to spend your hard-earned cash on (check out
the reward lists later in this book for some ideas) and you
really do *deserve* to enjoy the best that your money can buy.

2. A better sense of taste

Smoking deadens your taste buds and many successful stoppers find that they enjoy their food much more after quitting. Some get really into cooking and don't need to pour salt all over their food to appreciate subtle and delicious flavours.

3. A nicer smile

Smoking stains your teeth and gives you bad breath (yucky but true!). Stopping will mean that you can get your teeth cleaned and with regular brushing they'll stay that way. You'll have more to smile about when you've stopped for good and you'll avoid looking like the Wicked Witch of the West when you do!

4. Less stress

Smoking stresses you out and stopping calms you down once you've got through the withdrawal phase. Stopping will teach you to relax healthily and sleep more effectively so you'll be better able to cope with whatever life may have in store.

5. A longer life

Dying young, like James Dean or Jim Morrison, might sound glamorous when you're fourteen but as we get older most of us develop a healthy interest in staying alive! There's a lot of world out there to see and time is precious. You can add years to your life-expectancy by stopping smoking and you'll also improve the quality of life you can expect when you're older. These days so-called 'pensioners' are changing the rules about ageing and are getting much more out of life in their later years (just look at Joan Collins!) so there's a lot to look forward to if you can stay healthy for longer.

6. A more interesting life

Giving up smoking is boring. Yes, I know that might be a reckless thing for me to say, given that I'm asking you to read a book on the subject, but once you've learned all there is to know about it you don't want to have to go through the process again and again. Get on with it, get it right and you won't have to keep doing it year after year. You'll be free to take up the tuba, climb Mount Everest or crochet woolly hats, whatever 'floats your boat' so to speak. Get this job behind you and, unlike cooking or gardening, it will never need doing again.

7. Healthy kids

Research evidence about the effect of tobacco smoke on kids, health continues to pile up and it's not just in the womb that they suffer, it's in the home and throughout their childhood if one or both of their parents smoke. The effects include: cot death, being underweight at birth, glue-ear, asthma and respiratory problems. I won't labour this one as it's a bit of a 'downer' for any parent still smoking, but when you're smoke-free you won't have those worries any more and you'll be doing the best possible thing for your kids.

8. Confidence

Once you've successfully tackled tobacco addiction you really will be ready for anything! You'll have shown yourself that you can change your own behaviour and conquer something that's had you in its grip for years. You'll feel justifiably proud of yourself and you'll start to wonder what else you might be able to do if you put your mind to it. Stopping smoking won't turn you into a different person or give you miraculous powers but it will help you to realise your full potential.

9. Greater mobility

Smoking gradually restricts our mobility more and more over the years. It clogs up our lungs with tar and impairs our ability to breathe and get oxygen around the bloodstream. People who suffer from smoking-related diseases find that as time goes by they can do less and less. Some end up unable even to rise from a chair or breathe unaided. Human beings are meant to be able to walk, run, jump, skip and generally get about under their own steam and life can be pretty miserable if your mobility is under threat. We can't all be Lynford Christie or Pete Sampras but whatever your current level of mobility and independence, you'll get more out of life and enjoy it for longer if you stop smoking.

10. Helping others

When you stop smoking for good, you will be helping others to do it too, and in time this will add to your sense of satisfaction. If you have children you'll be showing them that tobacco addiction can be beaten and if you have a partner or a loved one who smokes your success may well be the spur that helps them to make the break too. There's nothing like seeing someone close to you succeed for making you realise that it really can be done.

11. Better sex!

Smoking is associated with infertility in women and impotence in men. It decreases the blood supply to the penis by up to a third and makes men more stressed, which also affects their sexual performance. Giving up smoking could put a spring in your step and the sizzle back in your sex-life ...

12. A better sense of smell

As a smoker your sense of smell is probably not very good. Once you stop you'll be able to smell your food, flowers, perfume and all manner of other aromas that passed you by before. You'll smell nicer to other people too, and your home and clothes will be cleaner and fresher.

The Health Benefits of Stopping

Many smokers want to know how their risk of contracting smoking-related diseases will fall once they stop. This varies from one illness to the next but to help you see the advantages here are a few of the main ones together with the time it takes for risk levels to drop compared with the situation for a 'continuing smoker' – 'CS':

Stroke – your risk reduces to that of a never-smoker 5 to 15 years after stopping

Cancers of the mouth, throat & oesophagus – risk halves compared to a CS

Coronary heart disease (the biggest killer of smokers) – the excess risk caused by smoking is halved compared to that of a CS just one year after stopping

Lung cancer – risk drops to 50% of that of a CS 10 years after stopping

Low birth-weight baby – risk drops to that of a never-smoker for women who stop before pregnancy or during the first 3 months

Remember: It's never too late to stop, but if you stop in middle-age (35–69) you'll avoid most of the risks of getting a serious smoking-related disease.

If you still need to build up motivation for the challenge of stopping smoking then try reading the case studies that follow. Two of the quitters featured, Linda Heyes and Danny Murphy, were ordinary addicted smokers. They both squared up to the task of quitting for good and made a success of it long-term. Their motivations were different but they both used a combination of incentives and reliable treatments to get it right. The third, Dave Allen, used to be a smoking icon. His stage persona was that of a chain-smoking, whisky-swilling comic genius, but he too came to realise that smoking was an unnecessary evil and managed to cut it out of his act and his life.

CASE STUDY 1:
Linda Heyes – Bull's-eye!

Leader of the pack

My first experience of smoking was at school, I was bullied into trying it by a girl called Carol who was twice my size! It's hard to believe now but I was actually very timid and so I was a bit of a target for bullies. Carol was the leader of a gang and she and the others took me down to a hidey-hole under the stage at school saying 'we've got something to show you'. Like a fool I went with them and then they said 'go on, have a smoke'. At first I refused but eventually I tried it. It was absolutely awful and I promptly went green and almost passed out!

Lighting up

I messed about with the occasional cigarette over the next few years but I didn't start smoking on a daily basis until I was about eighteen when I went to work at a factory that made lampshades. All the other girls in the factory smoked so of course we'd spend all our breaks puffing away and it really became part of my daily routine. My parents weren't very happy about my smoking but as they both smoked themselves there wasn't a whole lot they could say about it.

'Being pregnant didn't put me off'

I didn't really think about stopping at all until I was pregnant with my son. Lots of people told me that I should pack up as smoking was bad for the baby although there wasn't as much pressure to quit back then. Whenever one of my younger sisters got pregnant they went right off cigarettes each time but being pregnant didn't put me off at all. I sailed through my pregnancies and I felt so healthy it was unreal. I think that at that time the pressure from other people almost made me carry on, I just wasn't ready to consider quitting then I suppose. I knew I shouldn't be doing it but as it didn't make me feel ill or anything I just carried on.

Cold turkey?

I was about thirty when I first stopped smoking and it was for financial reasons. My first marriage had broken up and money was hard to come by. I'd set my heart on getting a freezer for the house but I just couldn't afford to get one and smoke as well. Having a goal was really helpful and I managed to stop completely. I bought a freezer on credit with the payments spread over six months. Unfortunately when the payments had all been made and the debt disappeared so did my resolve ... I'd just moved back to Manchester and I was on my own when it happened. I don't really know why I started again but I know I felt terribly guilty about it afterwards.

Risky business

The next time I thought about stopping was when I went to see my doctor. I was thirty-four at the time and I'd been taking the pill to help control my hormone levels. The doctor looked at my notes and pointed out that taking the pill and smoking made me a prime candidate for all sorts of problems, including heart trouble. I'd always been so healthy it didn't seem important to me at the time so I kept on smoking and taking the pill but it did make me think.

'Bob's heart attack knocked me for six'

The biggest change in my attitude to smoking came when my best friend's husband had a heart attack. It was totally unexpected and it knocked me for six. You see, we all used to get together at weekends and play darts in one another's houses, we were really good friends and we were all smokers. Bob wasn't the sort of person you'd expect to have a heart attack because he ate healthy foods and had quite a physical job as a mechanic but of course he did smoke like the rest of us. At

first he managed to stop smoking but then he had one cigarette because all of his mates smoked and soon he was back
on the cigs on a regular basis. About six weeks later he had
another heart attack and over the last few years he's had no
less than six heart by-pass operations. His wife Lynne didn't
give up straightaway, it took her a while to get her head round
it but she didn't smoke in front of Bob. Eventually she did stop
and after that I realised that if I carried on I'd be the odd one
out. My best friends had stopped and they'd been through a
terrible ordeal as a result of their tobacco smoking so obviously my attitude to it changed. I started to think that maybe
I should stop and once again I thought about the financial side
as well. I was spending about £25 a week on cigarettes and
when they announced on the budget that cigarettes were
going up to around £3.00 a packet I thought 'that's it, I've got
to stop!'

Driving ambition

It helped me to have a goal, something to work towards. The
first time it was the freezer and the second time it was driving.
I'd always wanted to learn to drive but it's very expensive to
have all the lessons and get a car. Anyway, I told myself that if
I could successfully give up smoking then I could afford to
have lessons and buy a car. That did it; I had a goal to strive for
and my mind was made up. I told everyone that I'd be packing
it in after Christmas. I didn't think it would be a good idea to do
it before because all the family would be coming and lots of
them smoke. I'm the eldest of six children and we're a very
close family so we do get together a lot. Christmas can be an
emotional time of year too so that was another reason for waiting until the New Year. After I'd made the decision to quit I
found myself looking at every cigarette I smoked and thinking
'I don't really want these', I suppose I kind of brainwashed
myself as time went by. I hadn't set an exact date for stopping
but as it happened I did stop on New Year's Day.

In the beginning I used some nicotine gum and that helped on the first day. I went and bought some at lunchtime and then had some more in the evening. On a difficulty scale of 1 to 10 that first day was an 11! It did start to get easier after that and by about the fifth day it was much better. I started to think "I'm less likely to have a heart attack now" and I knew that the risk would keep going down as long as I didn't smoke. My family were pretty supportive really but my brother's a bit of a comic and when we all went off on holiday together he'd say things like 'I'll keep this lighter for you for when you start again'.

Bull's-eye!

At the time when I gave up smoking I was captain of the ladies darts team at our local bar and I always used to play with a dart in one hand and a cigarette in the other. I thought that if I could get through that situation without smoking then I really could get through anything! Darts can get very competitive and before, if I was struggling to get a double, say to finish the match, I'd have a quick puff on a cigarette and bingo! I'd get my double. At first I wasn't sure if I'd be able to play at all without smoking but when it came to it there was no problem at all. I could play just as well as before and I didn't need a smoke to get me through a tight spot after all.

Third time lucky

After the darts match everything I did became a kind of challenge and I got to thinking that if I could beat tobacco then I might be able to do a whole lot of other things too. I'd always wanted to learn to drive so I started lessons and set myself the goal of passing the test and getting my own car. Maybe that won't sound like much to some people but for me it was a dream come true when I finally passed on my third attempt. It wasn't easy though and after I failed the second time I felt so disheartened I actually asked my examiner for a cigarette! Fortunately he said 'no way!' and told me not to give up on myself. Funnily enough, the day I passed my test was April 16th, Bob's birthday, so everything seemed to be connected in some strange way.

Hot stuff!

Since I stopped smoking my life has turned around completely. Because of being able to drive I'm earning 2 or 3 times as much money as I used to. I've got a lot more confidence now and a lot more freedom too. One of the biggest plusses is that I can taste things so much better now. I love food and cooking and the way my sense of taste came back was incredible. I used to eat curries before and I liked them medium to hot but now I can't stand them that hot, they burn my mouth. All of this goes to show how 'shot' my taste buds were when I smoked. I put on a bit of weight after stopping but not a lot and it seems to be coming off now so that's not a problem and I really notice that my breathing is easier. I used to get breathless running upstairs but not anymore.

Stop and go for it!

Both my children started smoking when they were quite young and my son still does but my daughter, Vicky, who still lives at home has managed to quit. She'd been seeing a young man and they'd just got engaged. They wanted to go away on holiday but couldn't really afford it so I said 'well, if you quit smoking you will be able to afford it'. At first Vicky said 'I can't, I haven't got your willpower' but I told her to go and book the holiday and pay the deposit, that way she was committed to stopping. That did it and although she found it hard at first she's still not smoking now, 12 months later – and they enjoyed a wonderful holiday together in Turkey.

If anyone out there is thinking about quitting I'd say go for it! Believe in yourself and you really *can* do it. Everybody daydreams about the things they want so you just have to use those dreams to motivate you and commit yourself to succeeding. If you want something badly enough then you'll do it.

LINDA'S TOP TIPS FOR SUCCESS

★ Choose a goal to help motivate you and commit yourself to it.
★ Choose your own time to stop and 'programme' yourself into believing that you don't really want to be a smoker any more in the run-up to your quit day.
★ Believe in yourself – you really can do it!

CASE STUDY 2:
Danny Murphy – Life in the Fast Lane!

Policeman Danny Murphy was a hardened smoker but he was finding it more and more difficult to keep up with the criminals on his patch! He knew that it was time to do something about his smoking habit so when his wife Sue promised him a brand new motor-bike Danny got into gear ...

Behind the bike sheds
Both my parents smoked but my mother gave up when I was very young, I don't remember why. Sadly my dad died of cancer when I was sixteen and I left home then.

I don't know if he got cancer because of smoking but it could well have been the cause.

I started smoking when I was eleven years old. I remember it was behind the bike sheds at school with my mates. We all tried it together, it was just part of the game, you know, everybody had a go. At first it was just the odd one here and there whenever I could cadge one off somebody but as the years went by I started spending my dinner money on cigarettes and by the age of sixteen I was definitely a regular smoker.

I was one of the lads!

At sixteen, I left home to join the army. As you'd expect my smoking went up as a result. It was easier to buy them because I was working and at last I was being treated as an adult. If I wanted to buy cigarettes I could buy them freely. There were no parents there to say anything or to try to stop me. Everyone smoked in the army of course. It was rare to meet someone who didn't. I suppose it was all part of the image of a beer-swilling, hard-smoking, womanising soldier! At sixteen I wanted to be accepted as one of 'the lads' so I adopted the whole lifestyle. When I went home on leave I smoked openly in front of my mum and she hit the roof but there wasn't anything she could do about it by that stage.

I smoked 'like a trooper' in Germany

Over the next few years my smoking generally crept up but where I was stationed made a big difference. When I was living in Germany I'd smoke 40 or even as much as 60 a day because cigarettes were so cheap. They were tax free, you see. I smoked all the major brands, whatever I could get my hands on at   the time.

My first attempt

I'd always prided myself on being fit and healthy because I had such an active lifestyle. I used to run 8 or 9 miles every day and I played a lot of sport. I think that was my downfall really. I believed that I could get away with smoking by being fit. It works for a while but as you get older it catches up with you. By the time I was twenty-four I was just past my physical peak and I found that because I was getting that little bit older I was struggling to go the extra mile. I wanted to get better at squash and go up a level but I just couldn't seem to get any fitter so I thought I'd try giving up smoking. I was stationed in Northern Ireland at the time.

My mate's shoelaces tripped me up ...

I gave up 'cold turkey' without any aids or anything and I did pretty well because I was working practically all the time and I didn't think about smoking while I was working. I lasted about three months but I 'came undone' in a plane on the way home from my tour of duty. I'll never forget it. My mate's shoelace was undone and he passed me his cigarette and said 'can you hold that while I do up my laces?'. I had it in my hand and took a puff. It was almost automatic and unfortunately I was back on 20 or 30 a day soon afterwards.

Stop! You're killing me

A few years later in 1989 I decided to have another go at stopping. It was partly because my wife had never smoked and although she didn't nag me about it I knew she'd be pleased if I stopped, because we'd started having children. Money was tight and I thought I should have a go for the sake of the family. Our eldest boy Stephen has always gone on about me smoking. He learned all about the health hazards at school and he'd come home and start opening all the windows. Then he'd start coughing and say things like, 'You shouldn't smoke indoors because we're getting it all in our lungs. You're killing me!' He could be a real pain about it to be honest but I had to admit that he had a point. I went cold turkey again but I only lasted a few days that time. It was harder than I'd thought it would be.

Slow cops and fast robbers!

My third and final quit attempt happened in 1997. I'd been in the police force for some time by then and I'd noticed that I was getting short of breath when I was running after people (villains!). It's no good being a slow-coach 'copper' running after speedy criminals so smoking was affecting my ability to do my job properly. I needed to be fit because my livelihood depended on it. The other reasons to stop were all there as well of course, the money and the family, so when my wife offered to buy me a brand new motor bike if I could stop for good that did it!

This time I used patches

I made the decision on Easter Sunday and smoked my last cigarette that night. I had cigarette supplies in the cupboard at home so I threw them all away and the next day I went to the chemists and bought some patches to help me. I found that they helped me psychologically by boosting my morale. I don't know how much they were helping physically but just knowing the patch was there made me feel better. I'd think 'I don't need a cigarette cos I've got a patch on'.

The first few days

On the first day I just got on with my normal day's work and I chewed a lot of gum (normal not nicotine) as it seemed to help to have something to do with my mouth.

I used the patches for about a week, then I used them alternate days for the second and third weeks. Then I stopped using them altogether. Some people were really encouraging saying things like, 'If you can do a day, you can do a week!' but others used to have a laugh and blow smoke at me! It didn't bother me too much though. I know they didn't really mean to be nasty and in the past I might have done the same thing myself.

The home straight

I think I found it easier at home because no one else smoked there anyway. It was harder at work, seeing other people having cigarette breaks. The worst point as far as the craving was concerned was the period from the middle of the first week to three-quarters through the second. After that it all started getting much easier. At the end of the third week it didn't really bother me much at all! I bought some nicotine chewing gum at that point and I used to carry the pack in my

pocket for those awkward moments when I would normally
have had a cigarette. As with the patches I found that it helped
my confidence to have something there for emergencies.

Happy families

My wife was really pleased that I'd stopped and so was
Stephen. I hadn't really believed that I'd get my new motor
bike, it seemed too good to be true, but in July of that year my
wife Sue told me to go and pick one out and that she'd buy it
for me. She took me to the shop and said 'choose whatever one
you want'. I felt like a kid in a sweet shop as you can imagine.
I'd had a bike in the past but I'd never had a new one before. I
chose a shiny green Honda CB500. It cost about £3,500 and I
was well impressed!

Now I don't smell and I've learned to cook!

Since I stopped smoking I've noticed that my life has improved
in lots of ways. I've got more money for one thing and I don't
smell anymore! During all my years of smoking I never
realised just how much I must have smelled of tobacco. These
days I can smell it a mile away on other people! My sense of
taste is far better too. I used to be a really picky eater, existing
on junk food mostly but these days I'm really into cooking and
I enjoy vegetables, foreign dishes and all sorts of things I'd
never have touched before. I've put on a little weight, about
half a stone, but that doesn't bother me at all. I've learned to
cook and eat properly so I really enjoy good food.

My sex-life has improved too!

They say that smoking doesn't do your love-life any favours
and in my case giving up certainly had a positive effect on it.
My wife never used to like it when I'd have a cigarette right
after we made love. She says it's 'afterwards' that matters as
well, so when I stopped smoking she thought it was a big
improvement. The other thing was that as soon as we got the

bike we took the opportunity to go away for romantic weekends together so it really did spice up our love-life when I gave
tobacco the heave-ho.

DANNY'S TOP TIPS FOR SUCCESS

★ Use a nicotine replacement product to help you, whether
  it's chewing gum, patches or whatever because the
  psychological help they give really is fantastic. They help
  you to believe that you don't need a cigarette.
★ Take one day at a time. Don't think, 'I'm never going to
  smoke again' just think, 'I'm not going to smoke today'.
  Set yourself realistic short-term goals; e.g. that you can do
  a day, a week, or 2 weeks. Then maybe you can do a
  month etc. etc.
★ Get rid of all your smoking stuff before you quit to avoid
  temptation. (I even threw away an expensive lighter I'd
  bought so as to avoid unnecessary temptation!)

CASE STUDY 3:
Dave Allen – Stopping for Good

My initiation into smoking

I had my first drag on a cigarette when I was six if I remember
right. All the kids around Dublin smoked so it was almost
inevitable that I would too. I had two brothers who did and that
certainly influenced me. Starting to smoke was a kind of initiation you see, a way of becoming part of a gang and there were
various different stages you had to go through before you
became a proper member.

Stage 1: The first drag

First you had to steal a cigarette from your ma or an aunt or
something. The first drag was hot and it tasted terrible but

you had to try it with your friends watching to make sure that you went through with it. This was a very unsophisticated attempt at smoking, it made you cough and splutter but it was a beginning.

Stage 2: Nasal skills
The next goal for the novice smoker was to learn to blow the smoke out of your nose. My first attempt at this wasn't very pretty, snot flew out of my nose and I had tears in my eyes but, like the others, I knew I had to do the macho thing and go through with it.

Stage 3: Holding it down
The third stage of the initiation was learning to inhale, which made you cough like crazy but once you'd mastered it you were almost there and when you could hold the smoke down for ages without exploding or being sick you knew that you'd finally made the grade and that you were a fully paid up 'Smoking Mason'!

I fell in love with the 'Goldflake' woman
Looking back I realise that over the years the tobacco ads have been very clever – they promoted the macho thing to us boys with all the connections with sport and strength and they attracted the girls with the chic, sophisticated stuff. I went to school in Dublin at a convent run by the Loreto nuns. Just opposite the school there was a laundry called the 'Swastika Laundry' (you don't see many of them these days!) and next to that was a big ad for Wolsey's Goldflake Tobacco which pictured a wonderful woman on a horse. I remember that ad so well. I fell in love with the wonderful Goldflake woman because she was very pretty. A manly looking chap was holding out a packet of cigarettes to her and that was the image: beautiful women and manly men enjoying the great outdoors! I was hooked in every sense.

Smoking on screen

When I was young the films certainly gave you the impression
that you could pull the birds if you smoked. I went to the
cinema every week and everyone in the movies smoked, especially the heroes. We copied smoking tricks learned from the
films; there was one actor who could throw a cigarette into his
mouth so we spent hours practising that and the other trick I
recall was being able to roll a cigarette from one side of your
mouth to the other, that seemed really cool at the time. The
villains (who were almost always German) smoked differently
from the English. The English were tight-lipped smokers, very
proper, whereas the Germans smoked with stiff military
movements and used holders. They often had monocles too,
so we played games, imitating them and the way they smoked.

We learned about sex from smoking in the movies

Back in the 40s and 50s smoking was definitely a substitute or
a metaphor for sex in the movies. People were heavily influenced by the new 'talkies' and cigarettes were used by the
actors to show wanton desire. They weren't allowed to be too
graphic because of the censors so they used smoking as a kind
of sexual language. Betty Davis could eat or seduce cigarettes
in a way that illustrated her moods. Offering someone a cigarette was like making a pass at them, stubbing one out fiercely
showed what a 'ball-breaker' she could be and lips were potent
symbols of sex too, especially when a man and woman lit each
other's cigarettes. As kids we practised 'chain lighting'. We'd
say, 'Put yours to mine and pull!', it was all sexual innuendo.
At that time you could get spring-loaded cigarette packets that
pushed a cigarette up really slowly; it was a clever gimmick
and it was all part of the smoking and mating game.

My father made us smoke fat Havana cigars

I felt guilty about smoking as a child. I loved my pa very much
and ordinarily I wouldn't have lied to him but smoking made

me both a liar and a thief. We used to chew scallions (onions) to mask the smell of smoke on our breath but he knew that we'd been smoking because no one would chew scallions for any other reason! He caught us at it once and made us smoke a whole load of fat Havana cigars but he didn't realise what hardened smokers we were so he was amazed when we managed to smoke them all without throwing up!

Nun but the brave...

Most of the priests I knew from my school days smoked and they often decided to give up for Lent. That meant that during Lent the physical punishments for our misdemeanours became ten times worse because all the priests were in a filthy mood! You were in fear of your life from those madmen sometimes! The nuns always seemed angry anyway but I don't think that was because they were quitting smoking.

My smoking day

It's true to say that I became a constant smoker, it was an ever-present feature of my waking existence. I'd smoke first thing in the morning and last thing at night. I'd have one in my mouth all the time and I'd smoke 60, 70, 80 a day, maybe more. I'd even shave and smoke at the same time. My girlfriend hated it, at one point she cut my cigarette in bits with scissors as it protruded from my lips! I had packets everywhere and I smoked with everything I did. It was a big part of my life. I smoked Gauloise – they seemed to be better cigarettes for some reason (if there is such a thing). I didn't like the smell of the other brands.

Excuses, excuses ...

When anyone questioned the wisdom of my smoking habit I had all those excuses like 'you've got to die somehow' etc. I used to ask people 'Do you mind if I smoke?' when I lit up and if they dared to say 'Yes' I was deeply indignant. I'd protest and say, "What do you mean? How dare you!" When my smokers' cough made me hack and splutter I'd always say I'd got a cold or a chest infection but of course I'd never blame it on the smoking.

Smoking and my work

I didn't consciously set out to make smoking a symbol of my performance but I liked to have a drink and a cigarette and I suppose I promoted a very relaxed form of comedy. I was allowed to smoke on TV and so people came to think of me with a fag in one hand and a drink in the other. I wasn't allowed to smoke on stage though, for safety reasons. I'd do a 2- or-3 hour show without smoking and it didn't actually bother me while I was up there doing the show. That started me thinking. I realised that when I was distracted I didn't need to smoke. I also like to paint in my spare time and when I was painting, I'd let fags burn away because I was concentrating. I began to think that maybe I could stop if I could find ways to distract myself. I'd started to think it might be an idea to stop because I had children and I didn't want them to start. I knew I wouldn't be able to say 'it's bad for you – don't do it' when I was doing it myself.

Playing games

I decided not to give up, but to cut down. The two sides of my addicted smoker's brain were working hard to find a way of appeasing my conscious without having to quit completely. 'It's not too bad' I thought as I lay in bed, 'I'll only smoke at certain times'. I worked it all out: I sleep for about 8 hours a day and I don't smoke then, so I've got 16 hours to play with. Bathing, eating and being in places where I couldn't smoke accounted for another 4 hours so I reckoned I could get by on about 12 cigarettes a day. As I planned it all out I lit a cigarette and then started to worry – it was 8.05 am and I'd only got 11 left! By noon I only had 4 left and I was really panicking! Only 4 left now – so I thought I'd borrow cigarettes from tomorrow's allowance on the basis that withdrawal wouldn't be so bad tomorrow. 'Maybe I'll only need 8 tomorrow' I thought eagerly, 'so I'll borrow 5 for today' ... I eventually worked myself into a cigarette debt that no one could ever pay and began to see that cutting down is a road to nowhere. At that point I decided to stop for good.

New York, New York...
One day I said 'That's it!' I was due to open a show in New York and people said 'you'll be under pressure, you're bound to crack up' but I didn't and I thought 'I don't need these bloody things anymore!' I haven't smoked at all since except accidentally in the course of filming a comedy sketch. I was playing the part of a bored bishop, listening to other bishops holding forth and I put a cigarette in my mouth and lit it as part of the act. I suddenly thought 'Oh my God, I've smoked!' and a nearby stage-hand said 'I thought you'd given up smoking'. That might have been a tricky moment looking back but it was a genuine mistake and I didn't crack up afterwards.

Russian roulette
I don't think it's really that difficult to stop once you make up your mind properly. I think a lot of it's in your head. The addiction creates all sorts of symptoms when you stop but it's in your mind too. Once you say 'these bastards are killing me', and realise that you're paying some greedy bastard to give you something that's going to kill you, the sheer lunacy of that situation brings it home to you. I'd say it's like playing Russian roulette with six bullets in the chamber – it is going to kill you! You only have to go into hospitals to see the way heavy smokers end up if they don't manage to stop.

One day at a time
I don't miss smoking at all now but I've had realistic relapse dreams in the past: I've dreamt that I've bought a cigarette, knowing I'm doing wrong and I've woken up convinced I've

had one – I actually look for the packet under my pillow! I don't know why I've had these dreams but I've heard that others have them too when they've stopped for good so maybe it's part of the process you go through. I think it's important to take it a day at a time, don't say never. It gets easier as you go along.

MY MESSAGE TO SMOKERS

★ Once your mind's made up, you really can give up smoking.
★ Don't betray yourself and don't let all those silly excuses make you break your word to yourself.
★ Just try it and it'll get easier and easier with every day that passes.

If I can do it anyone can so good luck to you!

CHAPTER 3

Know the Enemy!

Any good general would tell you that if you're going into battle, it pays to know as much as possible about the enemy you're going to be up against and the same is true if you're preparing to fight tobacco addiction. Knowledge is power, and the more you understand about the nature of tobacco addiction the more likely you are to be able to beat it for good. You might call this chapter 'The Science Bit' as it contains factual information about the nature of tobacco addiction but it's not too heavy (I promise) and it's essential reading if you're serious about stopping.

WHAT'S IN A CIGARETTE?

Many smokers (and quite a few health professionals) would be quite hard put to it to tell you exactly what you take into your body when you smoke a cigarette, so let's get that as clear as we can.

The contents of cigarette smoke are as follows:

1. **Nicotine** (a drug that is highly addictive when inhaled in tobacco smoke)
2. **Carbon monoxide** (a poisonous gas created when something is burned)
3. **Tar** (nasty brown residue that clogs up your lungs)
4. **4000 chemicals** (including pesticides and known poisons)

Nicotine, friend or foe?

Most smokers now know that cigarettes contain nicotine and that nicotine is an addictive drug but many are confused about the contents of cigarette smoke and which chemicals actually do the most damage. Perhaps the most important thing to stress here is:

STOP PRESS! – NICOTINE DOESN'T CAUSE CANCER!

I'm highlighting this point as much as possible because a lot of people fear that it does and avoid products that contain nicotine for this reason. A few years ago scientists finally established that inhaling nicotine in tobacco smoke was highly addictive. Unfortunately, because we fear 'addiction' and associate it with so-called 'hard' drugs like heroin and cocaine, nicotine got branded as the 'bad guy' in the smoking story, whereas it's really all the other stuff in tobacco smoke that hurts you, nicotine just keeps you puffing! The invention of Nicotine Replacement Therapy (NRT) which allows smokers to satisfy their craving for the drug whilst avoiding all the harmful stuff in tobacco smoke was a major breakthrough in research into stopping smoking. It has helped thousands of smokers to quit but, sadly, people are so frightened by nicotine's image as an 'addictive drug' that many are fearful of using it! These days only about 25% of those who try to stop smoking each year take advantage of NRT which is a crying shame when it could double or even treble their chances of succeeding.

So, how come nicotine is so bad in cigarettes and yet OK in patches or gum? The answer to this question could be summed up by saying:

'It ain't what you take it's the way that you take it!'

because although nicotine is an addictive substance, it's addictive power depends on the speed with which it reaches the brain and how often it is sent there.

'Puffology'

Each puff on a cigarette delivers a powerful 'burst' of nicotine to your brain within 3 or 4 seconds, that's even faster than if you were to inject it into a vein! There are about 10 puffs in each cigarette so for a 20-a-day smoker that's 200 regular drug hits a day ... Day after day, week in and week out, smokers get totally accustomed to this pattern. The nicotine hits their brains time after time and the sensation it produces becomes intimately associated with practically everything they do in their waking hours. That's why smoking seems such an indispensable part of daily life to regular smokers and why the first day without a cigarette can seem as strange as a walk on the moon.

HOW TOBACCO ADDICTION WORKS

For a drug to be classed as highly addictive (like heroin or crack cocaine for example) it has to do two things: Firstly it has to give you a strong 'hit' to the brain pretty swiftly. Secondly, it needs to stop giving you that hit or satisfaction soon after you stop taking it. That way you start enjoying the hit but then it soon goes away, leaving you wanting more. It's like an itch that can never be properly scratched because the more you do it the more you need to, and so on. The nicotine you take in from tobacco smoke reaches your brain very quickly, but then it leaves almost as fast, so even as you stub out your last cigarette, your need for the next one is starting to build up. This 'quick in – quick out' pattern is what makes tobacco addiction so very powerful. Most of the time we're unaware of it but after a while it makes us believe that we simply can't manage without that regular nicotine hit and we have to keep those cigarettes coming, day in and day out, packet after packet, puff after puff.

Just a bad habit?

Some smokers resist the idea that they're actually addicted. No one likes to feel that they're in the power of some controlling

drug addiction, which dominates their behaviour, so this attitude is fairly understandable. They may put the whole thing
down to habit. Long-term smokers will argue that they can't
stop because they've done it all their lives and the habit is too
'ingrained' to be changed now. Sounds persuasive? Yes, but the
fact remains that if we removed all the nicotine from their cigarettes they'd soon notice that something was wrong! Smoking
without nicotine is a completely pointless activity because it
gives the smoker no drug 'reward'. Without nicotine a cigarette
is about as useful to a smoker as a chocolate teapot! All that
hand-to-mouth stuff and the business about wanting something to do with your hands at parties is relatively unimpor-
tant compared to the effect of nicotine on a smoker's
behaviour. Smokers are addicted to nicotine and that's what
keeps them smoking even though they know it's bad for them.
Tobacco companies are very clever at putting just the right
amount of nicotine in cigarettes to get people addicted and
keep them that way so don't ever feel that it's your fault you
got hooked. The modern cigarette is just about the most effective drug delivery device known to man and tobacco companies don't spend billions of pounds marketing their products
for nothing. They know how to make the most of the addictive
nature of tobacco and unless you do something about it they'll
make a nice fat profit from your inability to escape from it.

Taking your nicotine 'clean'

Products like nicotine patches and gum also deliver nicotine
into your body and brain but they do it in a gentle, gradual
way by being absorbed slowly through the skin. They help to
reduce craving and withdrawal symptoms while you learn to
do without the succession of 'nicotine hits' that was normal to
you when you smoked. It doesn't take long for the pattern of
repeated hits to be broken and after a few weeks most people
are ready to reduce their nicotine dose and then come off
it altogether.

Q. What if I can't stop using a nicotine replacement product?

A. The vast majority of ex-smokers who've used NRT (Nicotine Replacement Therapy) find it fairly easy to wean themselves off it after a few weeks. It contains much less nicotine than cigarettes and isn't nearly so addictive but even if you stayed on it for the rest of your life the chances are that it wouldn't do you any harm at all, unlike cigarettes:

Carbon monoxide gas

Cigarette smoke also contains lots of carbon monoxide gas (the same stuff that comes out of car exhaust pipes!) and it's this gas that causes heart and circulation problems in long-term smokers. It dissolves in your blood much faster than oxygen and attaches itself to your red blood cells where the oxygen should be. This is bad news for two main reasons:

1. Your heart has to work much harder in order to get enough oxygen round your body. Over the years this puts a great strain on your heart and that's why so many smokers die of heart attacks at a relatively young age. Their hearts just couldn't take the strain any more.

2. Too much carbon monoxide in your bloodstream makes it thicker and stickier and more likely to form dangerous clots.

Hypercarboxyhaemoglobinaemia (HCHB)

This impossibly long-sounding condition is caused by having too much carbon monoxide (CO) in your bloodstream and the term was coined by STOP! Magazine's Resident Doctor Chris Steele who firmly believes that doctors should routinely test their patients for HCHB. It's really easy to check what your CO levels are by using a gadget called a CO Monitor or 'Smokerlyser'. You just hold your breath for 15 seconds, then blow it all into the machine's mouthpiece through a cardboard tube.

Within a few seconds you get a digital readout showing the level of CO gas in your blood at the time. Non-smokers usually get readings of less than 10 (we all have a little CO in our blood because of pollution etc.) but if you've smoked in the hours leading up to the test then the reading will almost certainly be higher than 10. Regular 20-a-day smokers often get readings of 20 to 30, whilst heavier smokers can get up to 30, 40 or 50. The highest I've seen was a reading of 125 in a 60-a-day chain smoker! All of this sounds most alarming at first but within just a couple of days of stopping CO levels drop right down to normal and it's very encouraging to see the difference after working your way through the first few days without cigarettes. Taking the test *before* you stop smoking will help you to gauge your level of nicotine dependence and taking it *after* you've stopped will give you real proof that what you're doing is working. Some health centres and clinics already have CO Monitors so it's possible to go along and ask for a test or, failing that, you could ring your local health promotion or health education department for advice on where to go.

Tar
Also known as TPM (total particulate matter), tar is the disgusting black gooey stuff that gets left behind in your lungs if you smoke. I don't propose to go on about it because it's too revolting and we've probably all seen pictures of blackened lungs etc. in the past. Suffice to say that it's rather like the stuff that collects in the sump of a car and isn't at all the sort of thing that you want in your body ... Once you stop smoking your body will have a jolly good go at clearing it out and, depending on how much is in there, it will succeed to some degree. The human body is an amazingly sophisticated 'machine' and has fantastic powers of recovery if you give it a chance to demonstrate them so don't despair. We're all born with a kind of 'respiratory cleaning system' which consists of lots of tiny hairs called 'cilia'. These little hairs line our respiratory passages

and help to waft impurities up and out of our upper airways (chest, nose and throat). Smoking completely destroys this delicate mechanism, but once you stop, it reactivates and begins, slowly but surely, to remove the unwanted matter from your lungs. It takes time and can result in your chest feeling even more 'gurgly' for a while but it's a healing process and 'it's better out than in' as they say!

4000 chemicals

It may sound incredible but there really are this many trace chemicals in tobacco smoke. We hardly know what all of them are because the tobacco manufacturers aren't obliged to tell us (in addition to the fact it would be rather hard to list them all on the packet.). We do know that they include toxic substances such as lead, cyanide, arsenic, pesticides and many known carcinogens (things that cause cancer). We live in a world of sophisticated consumers, we check the labels on our food and worry about mad cow disease and genetically modified foods, but when it comes to tobacco it seems that anything goes. The tobacco manufacturers can put the nastiest things imaginable in their products because they are so addictive, and by smoking we'll take stuff into our bodies that we wouldn't use to clean the car or spray on the weeds in our gardens! Heaven knows what this 'toxic cocktail' does to our bodies over the years, it doesn't really bear thinking about, so the best idea is to get on with the business of stopping as soon as possible.

TWO ADDICTIONS FOR THE PRICE OF ONE

If you're a regular smoker then you're addicted to tobacco in two different ways: **Physically** and **Psychologically**. You're going to need to tackle these addictions simultaneously when you stop and that means having plans and strategies for both. We've already looked at some of the physical processes involved but the psychological side is very important too. The more you understand about the ways in which it affects your behaviour and your thought patterns the less likely it is that you'll be fooled by a bit of classic 'addictive thinking' or 'tobacco logic'.

The smoking club

The psychological role that it plays is such that, over the years, smoking becomes a big part of our identity. (See case studies pages 19–35.) We see ourselves as smokers and we spend a lot of time with other smokers. This isn't because they're such a wonderful subset of humanity but because they're the people who are around when we go to the smoking room at work for a break. We meet them when we're skulking around the back of the building having a crafty puff and when we spend long hours in smoky pubs. By getting addicted to tobacco we've joined a club and all the members of this club behave in similar ways. Smoking restrictions throw members of this 'club' together because they can only get the hit they need in certain places and of course they all sympathise with one another because they all feel a bit 'got at' by non-smokers and all their rules and regulations. The 'brotherhood' of smokers sounds great doesn't it, 'all for one and one for all', 'united we stand' etc. etc., but unfortunately its members have something else in common: most of them will die younger, sicker and sadder because of their addiction. The 'camaraderie' of the smoking club falls apart when the going gets tough and isn't to be relied on if you get sick. Fellow club members don't want to be reminded of what they've got to look forward to if they carry on so they may give you a wide berth at that stage.

Leaving the club

When you decide to give up smoking you also have to leave the 'smoking club' we've been talking about and this can be very worrying at first. Your mind may race ahead thinking of all sorts of problems and reasons why you can't possibly renounce your lifelong membership: What will happen to your social life after you stop? Will you have to avoid all your smoking friends and make new ones? Where will you go on work breaks and will everyone think that you've deserted your smoking brothers and sisters? It may seem very frightening when you think about 'going it alone' and your fear is understandable but you can stop smoking without becoming a social leper or losing all your friends – and there are ways to cope without resorting to cigarettes. Within a few short weeks you will have adapted to a slightly different daily routine and your friends will have accepted that you no longer smoke. Some of the smokers amongst them will envy your success, others may make jokes about it to wind you up, but after a while it will cease to be an issue. Life will be back to normal except for one important difference: You won't be smoking anymore.

CHAPTER 4

Know Yourself

At the beginning of the last chapter I said that if you're going in to battle you need to know lots about the enemy but you also need to know a good deal about yourself; your strengths, weaknesses etc. etc. If you want to change something about your behaviour then you need to analyse it a bit first to find out if it follows any kind of predictable pattern. Smoking is, in many ways a very predictable behaviour that is certain to involve a reasonably regular pattern of daily activity but all smokers vary and some are more dependent on nicotine than others. In this chapter I'm going to show you how to find out how nicotine dependent you really are and how to look for patterns in your daily smoking routine that will help you to plan your stopping strategies and avoid relapsing later on.

WHAT SORT OF SMOKER ARE YOU?

Before you stop smoking it's helpful to get an idea of just how dependent on nicotine you really are. If you're heavily addicted, for example, then you're more likely to benefit from stronger forms of Nicotine Replacement Therapy such as 4mg gum, 15mg patches or Nicotine Nasal Spray, whereas lighter smokers may be fine with 2mg gum or medium strength patches (10mg). If possible you should get your carbon monoxide levels checked. This will give a good indication of how much you take in from the cigarettes you smoke, but in the meantime why not try this quick and easy DIY Dependence Test: just answer the questions and then check your score. The higher the score, the more dependent you are.

The DIY Nicotine Dependence Test

1. It's 7am – your alarm has just gone off and you know it's time to get up, do you:
    (a) get ready for work, leave the house and wait until later to start smoking.
    (b) make breakfast, eat it and then have a cigarette.
    (c) get up, make a cup of tea or coffee and then light up.
    (d) open your eyes and reach out for your fag packet and lighter immediately.

2. How many cigarettes do you normally smoke in a day?
    (a) 10 or less
    (b) 11 to 20
    (c) 21 to 30
    (d) 31 or more

3. You're out to dinner with a non-smoker at a posh restaurant. The service is slow and you're dying for a cigarette, do you:
    (a) wait politely, enjoy the meal and conceal your desire to smoke.
    (b) gobble down your food at breakneck speed in order to have a smoke at the end of the meal.
    (c) excuse yourself and pop out to the restrooms/ toilets for a quick one.
    (d) light up anyway and smoke between courses.
    (e) light up anyway and smoke between mouthfuls and between courses!

4. It 's 11.30 in the evening, it's pouring with rain and blowing a gale. You've only got one cigarette left and you

want to smoke it now but if you do you won't have any for the morning, do you:

(a) resist the desire to smoke it and go to bed.

(b) smoke it, go to bed and plan to buy more cigarettes in the morning.

(c) smoke half of it, put it out and save the rest for the morning, reasoning that a second-hand smoke will be better than nothing.

(d) put on your coat and walk half a mile to the all-night garage for another packet so that you can smoke as much as you want now and in the morning.

5. You've just come down with a bad chest infection and are laid up in bed, your doctor has advised you to quit smoking immediately, do you:

(a) stop smoking for a couple of days to help your chest recover.

(b) cut down and feel very virtuous but extremely sorry for yourself.

(c) continue smoking as much as ever and put up with your hacking cough on the grounds that the stress of quitting will actually make you worse and the doctor just doesn't understand.

(d) smoke even more than usual as a result of feeling so ill and depressed about smoking!

Scoring system:
Your answers will be worth the following number of points:
   a = 0, b = 1, c = 2, d = 3, e = 4

What your score indicates:
0 to 5 – You are a fairly light smoker and you are usually able to refrain from smoking for short periods when necessary. You would probably benefit from 'lighter' forms of Nicotine Replacement such as 2mg gum or maybe the 'Inhalator' but it's

important not to be complacent about your low score as smokers tend to become more dependent as time goes by. You may become more addicted if you don't stop soon but on the plus side you may find that your physical cravings won't be too difficult to cope with if you make the break from tobacco sooner rather than later.

6 to 11 – You are a regular, dependent smoker with an established addiction to nicotine. If you decide to use NRT you may well find that 15mg patches or 4mg gum give you about the right amount of nicotine to reduce your cravings and you should think about stopping soon before your health suffers too much.

12 to 16 – You are clearly a hardened nicotine addict who finds it hard to refrain from smoking for long! You will probably need to try stronger forms of NRT to counteract your cravings after stopping, such as the Nicotine Nasal Spray or maximum strength patches. You really should try and get your carbon monoxide levels checked as a further indication of your dependence level and don't put off stopping for too long or your health may start to deteriorate.

SMOKING PATTERNS

Now that you know a bit more about the extent of your dependence on nicotine it's time to have a look at the way you smoke day to day. If you want to change an ingrained, daily behaviour like smoking then you must first find out as much as possible about any patterns of use that are a recurrent feature of that behaviour. Although a great many smokers puff away at regular intervals throughout the day, some smoke more in the early part of the day whilst others really get serious in the afternoons and evenings. Work restrictions, individual preferences and the company we keep can all play a part in establishing our smoking routines, and the more you can find out about your own smoking patterns now, the better able you'll be to devise good relapse prevention strategies for use later on.

Fill out a smoking diary

By filling out the following diary on a 'typical smoking day' you'll discover when, where and how often you smoke, but also what moods and feelings prompt you to light up and whether there are particular 'triggers' or situations that will be especially hard to cope with when you stop. Carry the book around with you and be sure to note every cigarette you smoke at the time or you may forget some of the details. It's probably best to fill it in on a weekday as, for most of us, weekdays are more representative of normal daily routines.

How to complete your smoking diary

Time –make a note of the time of day at which you had each cigarette

Activity – summarise what you were doing at the time e.g. writing, chatting.

Mood – how did you feel just before you lit up? Bored? Angry? Happy? Write it down.

Who were you with? e.g. Friend, Boss, No one (sometimes just being with a particular person can make you want to smoke).

Where – where were you, in the pub, at home etc.

How much wanted/needed – write down how much you wanted or felt you needed each cigarette on a scale of 1 to 10 where 1 = not at all and 10 = desperately!

NB: I've allowed enough spaces here for 60 cigarettes per day but if you smoke more than that just continue on another piece of paper with the same headings. (Having to actually write something down can sometimes make the vital difference to your ultimate success in it and may confirm your resolve.)

YOUR SMOKING DIARY

TIME	ACTIVITY	MOOD	WHO WITH	WHERE	HOW MUCH WANTED (1-10)

TIME	ACTIVITY	MOOD	WHO WITH	WHERE	HOW MUCH WANTED (1-10)

Analysing your completed diary

Once you've filled in your smoking diary, you can analyse it and get some helpful tips for later on. Firstly have a look at how often you smoked. Did you smoke more than you thought or less, or the same as you imagined? Many smokers tend to 'round down' when they estimate their consumption so it's as well to investigate the truth of the matter! Check also in which periods of the day you smoke the most. You may be a regular 'every 30 minutes' smoker or you may smoke more in the latter part of the day. Whatever the situation in your case, be aware that the time points when you were most accustomed to smoking are likely to be a bit more problematic. Now look for particular situations when you smoked. Which were the cigarettes that you felt you really needed or wanted the most? After meals, on workbreaks and first thing in the morning are classic examples of 'much-wanted cigs' but you may find that there were other situations in which the urge to smoke was very strong. Identify your top ten dangerous situations, write them down and then refer to the lists of tips for coping with stress and cravings in Chapter 8 of this book. Writing down some helpful tips and suggestions next to your top ten list will help you to remember what to do when craving strikes later on. The more options you have in a given situation, the greater the chance that you'll come through it unscathed (i.e. without smoking!).

THE SAFER SMOKING MYTH

Most people's number 1 reason for wanting to stop smoking is to avoid unpleasant health problems and an untimely death, although money often comes a close second. Smokers who are considering quitting for good are often very anxious about stopping abruptly, so it can be extremely tempting to settle for a half-way option which promises some reduction in health risks, but allows you to carry on smoking. Two of the most common choices for people wanting to reduce their health risks without giving up altogether are:

1. switching to so called 'light' cigarettes (which claim to have lower tar, carbon monoxide and nicotine yields).
2. cutting down on the number of cigarettes smoked per day.

The big 'BUT' ...

Unfortunately there is now very good evidence (much of which is not widely known to the public) that these strategies will result in a much smaller reduction in health risk than the smoker expects, and in many cases may not reduce the health risks at all.

Why 'light' cigarettes are just as deadly

Cigarettes marketed as 'light', 'mild' or 'ultra light' are reported to deliver lower quantities of tar (the substance that causes cancer and respiratory illnesses) and nicotine (the addictive drug which people smoke for) than regular cigarettes. But have you ever wondered how the tobacco companies estimate this 'tar yield' for different types of cigarettes?

People don't smoke like machines

The figures given on cigarette packets are actually based on the results obtained when the cigarettes are smoked in a 'standard manner' by a machine. The key problem here is that, unsurprisingly, human beings don't smoke cigarettes in 'a standard manner' like machines. In the past you will probably have found that you smoke some of your cigarettes intensively almost right down to the butt. This might happen if you've been in a place where smoking wasn't possible (e.g. in an exam or in church) and your need for a cigarette has built up over time. At other times, in places where you can smoke as much as you want (e.g in the bar), you may have found that you puff far less on each cigarette and sometimes even allow them to burn out in the ashtray.

You have control

Regular smokers are experts at extracting the nicotine they need from the cigarettes available and they may not even be aware that they are doing it. In effect, smokers have complete control over the amount of smoke they inhale from each cigarette just by sucking harder and inhaling more often and more deeply. As a result, the number of cigarettes smoked per day is less important than you might imagine. It's what you get out of each cigarette that counts and this can be measured using a Carbon Monoxide Monitor or 'Smokerlyser'. To give you an example of this process in action, a typical 20-a-day smoker might get a 'CO' reading of, say, 25 parts per million (ppm). This shows that there is a lot more carbon monoxide gas in their blood than would be the case in a non-smoker (non-smokers usually get readings below 10 ppm). If the same smoker then cut down to 10 cigarettes per day then you might expect their reading to fall by 50% but it would probably only go down to about 20, showing that they had adapted to the new situation by extracting more from the cigarettes available. This shows that our 'regular smoker' can maintain the level of nicotine in his blood that he's used to, even if he reduces the number of cigarettes he smokes or switches to a lower nicotine brand.

'Holy' smoke!

The main method used by cigarette manufacturers to reduce the machine-smoked yields of cigarettes is to put tiny holes in the filter (vents) which allow air to be mixed with smoke when a person (or a machine) draws a puff. However, it's now clear that smokers who switch to these "light" cigarettes quickly learn to smoke them in a way that increases the amount of smoke they inhale, so that it is way above the machine-smoked yields printed on the packs. Smokers often do this by physically blocking the little holes with their lips or fingers and squeezing the filter a bit more than usual to cover them up. Putting the holes in the middle of the filter (exactly where you'd expect people to hold the cigarette) probably makes it more likely that the holes will get blocked and so makes them even less effective in reducing tar and nicotine intake.

Don't be fooled by the numbers game

A recent report by smoking expert Professor Lynn Kozlowski in the US has shown that Silk Cut Ultra (Lights) actually contain more nicotine (15.7mg) than Silk Cut Extra Mild (10.8 mg) and ordinary strength Silk Cut (13.8 mg). So the numbers printed on the packs (in this case 0.2mg nicotine for Silk Cut Ultra, and 0.5mg nicotine for regular Silk Cut) bear very little relation either to the total quantity contained in the cigarette or the total quantity absorbed by the smoker.

Don't put it off, put it out!

A recent study by the Health Education Authority revealed that 36% of smokers of 'light'cigarettes thought them to be less harmful than regular brands and about a quarter believed that switching to light cigarettes was a step towards quitting. Unfortunately the evidence suggests that 'light' cigarettes are just as harmful as regular varieties, and that for many smokers, switching to 'lights' merely delays the day when the person quits completely. Of course, the tobacco industry has known all of this for more than twenty years. An internal memo within the Philip Morris tobacco company in 1976 indicated that their own research on Marlboro Lights already showed that smokers of light cigarettes do not inhale less harmful smoke. It stated, *'The smoker profile data reported earlier indicated that Marlboro Lights cigarettes were not smoked like regular Marlboros. There were differences in the size and frequency of puffs, with larger volumes taken on Marlboro Lights...In effect, the Marlboro 85 (Lights) smokers in this study **did not achieve any reduction** in the smoke intake by smoking a cigarette normally considered lower in delivery.'*

Far from 'coming clean' about this knowledge in public, the industry chose to continue to con the public with the myth of the 'safer cigarette'. This strategy was revealed in a later BAT document, which summarised the industry's approach to marketing by stating:

> 'All work in this area should be directed towards providing consumer reassurance about cigarettes and the smoking habit. This can be provided in different ways, e.g. by claimed low deliveries, by the perception of low deliveries and by the perception of mildness.'

The main message for consumers is that if they are interested in doing something to reduce or avoid the health risks of smoking, then switching to so called 'light' cigarettes won't necessarily help achieve that aim.

Will cutting down help?

Some smokers try to cut down the number of cigarettes they smoke per day as a way of stopping smoking, or as a way of continuing to smoke with lower health risks. Cutting down gradually works for some people, but the evidence in favour of it is not very strong. In many ways it simply delays the point at which it really gets difficult (i.e. when you get to zero cigarettes per day). It has also been suggested that as you cut down to low levels (e.g. less than 5 per day) then each one becomes more reinforcing because you have spent so much time looking forward to it, and really enjoy each one as a result. However, so long as you actually get down to zero per day, and stick to it, you have achieved your aim just as surely as someone who gave up all at once.

Unfortunately, a more common pattern is to decide to get down and stay at a relatively low level (e.g. from over 20 per day to 10 or less). Again, the evidence is clear:

(a) the majority of people who do this soon get back up to their previous levels;

(b) even those who succeed in reducing the number of
cigarettes they smoke per day tend to inhale much more
smoke from each one than they previously did (again, in a
subconscious attempt to get their usual dose of nicotine).
In one study by Professor Neil Benowitz in the USA,
people who normally smoked an average of 37 cigarettes
per day were restricted to only five per day for four days.
It turned out that they inhaled three times as much

'I roll my own and I only smoke one a day'

smoke from each cigarette, and so only cut down their smoke exposure by about half, rather than by the 86.5% which would be expected based on the number of cigarettes. Given the possibility that you can get 3 times as much smoke from each cigarette by puffing more intensively, this means that a pack-a-day smoker would have to cut down to less than 7 per day to be sure that they had reduced their intake of smoke sufficiently.

I have seen many patients who made a determined attempt to cut down and some succeeded for as long as a few months. However, when some life stress came along, the cigarettes were still handy, and both the habit and addiction still strong, and so 5 per day very quickly became 10 and then 20. It does not have to happen like this but in my experience it frequently does. My view is therefore that the amount of effort it takes to maintain reduced smoking for ever is even greater, and the rewards far less, than quitting smoking altogether.

CHAPTER 5

Which Treatment?

These days smokers who want to quit are virtually bombarded with advertising for a whole range of treatments each promising to make stopping easier and grant them a passport to long-term success. Unless you've made a real study of the science it's difficult to know which products really work and which are just hype.

Bogus treatments

Smokers are quite naturally somewhat suspicious and cynical about handing over money for yet another 'miracle cure' when they're already spending so much on cigarettes but the desire to escape from tobacco and worsening health problems drives many to try all manner of weird and wonderful 'treatments'. Unfortunately there are some bogus and completely ineffective products out there and unscrupulous manufacturers who will take your money and who won't care whether you succeed or fail so long as they stand to gain in financial terms.

Effective treatments

On the other hand there are also some very good treatments that will make stopping easier if used correctly. The task is clear. Find out which products work and which don't and check how to get the best out of those that do. That's what this chapter is all about. The information given here is not based on my personal opinion or past experience but on the science of 'cessation' and on the huge amount of research that's been done on this subject in the last thirty years. This research has involved countless thousands of quitters in independent clinical trials all over the world. I've tried to cover most of the treatments that smokers will have heard about, but if you run into a therapy or a programme that is not mentioned here you can use the guide on p. 88 (Before you make your choice ...) to assess whether it's worth trying.

Nicotine Replacement Therapy

We'll begin this section with the group of treatments that go under the heading of NRT – Nicotine Replacement Therapy. If you've read the book this far you'll know that this is a treatment that I recommend, but getting the best out of it does mean that you have to use it properly. Lots of people will say that they've tried gum or patches and that they didn't work, but this often has more to do with *how* they used it than with the product itself. Don't dismiss NRT if you've tried it before as you may not have given it a chance to work properly. Read the information that follows and if, at the end of this section, you are still sure that you used it properly then I take it all back; if not, then maybe, just maybe, you ought to give it another try ...

A short history of NRT
Back in the 1960s the Swedish military noticed that the men on their submarines became irritable when they were unable to smoke. Smoking was of course banned on submarines and the men often became short-tempered and easily distracted while at sea (not a very good thing in an enclosed space as you may well imagine). A Swedish scientist, Ove Ferno, realised that it was the nicotine in cigarettes that the sailors were missing and so set out to find a way of providing nicotine without

tobacco. This was a real challenge as it's not easy to manipulate an unstable compound like nicotine but eventually Ferno cracked the problem and invented the first ever Nicotine Replacement Product in the form of gum. Ove Ferno was therefore the founding father of NRT and became the Head of Research at Pharmacia & Upjohn who now manufacture the Nicorette range of NRT products in the UK.

Tried and tested

Since its invention the various different forms of NRT have been tested again and again by independent research teams all over the world and there is now indisputable evidence that it doubles people's chances of stopping smoking successfully. It's not a magic cure, however, and needs to be used in combination with other non-drug strategies for it to work. The biggest problem is often that people don't use enough NRT to help with cravings or that they don't use it for long enough and relapse quickly when they stop using it too soon.

The cost of NRT

Although it's sometimes argued that smokers can afford NRT if they can afford to smoke, in reality it's often difficult to stump up the cost of a week's supply all in one go. In the future we hope that the government will make it easier for people to afford NRT products but if you can possibly afford it now it's a good health investment and you'll only be spending money on it for a few weeks. After that you won't need to buy NRT or cigarettes so in the longer term you'll be much better off all round.

Is it safe?

At the moment there are warnings on most NRT products which say that if you are pregnant or if you have heart disease then you should consult a doctor before using NRT. This doesn't mean that you can't use it but that you need to weigh up the pros and cons carefully. A regular 20-a-day smoker takes in a lot more nicotine from smoking than they would from using an NRT product instead so they would be better off with the latter even if they were pregnant or had heart disease. A very light smoker could get more nicotine from NRT than from low level smoking so you could argue that they shouldn't use it but, once again, if it helps them to quit tobacco they'll be much healthier in the long run. The bottom line is that the makers of NRT are being responsible when they advise some people to check with their doctors but the decision is yours. Smoking is terribly dangerous and NRT is not, so use your common sense on this issue. Check your level of dependence with our DIY test and read this guide to be sure of choosing the treatment plan that's best for you.

NICOTINE GUM

Nicotine gum comes in two flavours (mint or original) and two strengths (2mg or 4mg). Heavier smokers should choose the 4mg gum and lighter smokers should be OK with the 2mg variety but whatever type you choose you must use enough of it! Lots of would-be quitters fail because they simply don't use enough gum and so don't get enough nicotine into their blood. The gum can't help with cravings unless you give it a chance to build up the amount of nicotine in your bloodstream little by little so if you want to succeed you've got to use around 10 to 15 pieces a day in the first few weeks after stopping. Don't tell yourself that you're doing well if you 'only had a couple of pieces this morning'. In this case it doesn't pay to be cheese-paring and there is no great virtue in making yourself put up with more cravings than necessary.

You can't just chew!
When you use nicotine gum it's not like chewing Wrigleys. When you chew it, the nicotine is released into your mouth

and then absorbed through its lining. If you chew it too much you'll release too much too soon. The nicotine will be swallowed (probably giving you hiccups!) and swallowed nicotine isn't absorbed well so it is just wasted: so take it easy. Chew it a bit and then rest it against your cheek for a few minutes before having another go.

An acquired taste

When you first start using nicotine gum it tastes strongly of nicotine and can give you a sore throat. Don't be put off! If you chew it correctly then these side-effects will soon pass (probably within a day) and you'll soon learn to appreciate just how much it can help.

PROS

★ With gum it's easy to control your dose to suit your level of addiction
★ Chewing can be fun!
★ It can help to stop you eating too much
★ It gives you extra help in tough situations
★ It gives you something to do with your hands and mouth when craving strikes
★ It's possible to use it long-term

CONS

★ You might not use enough of it
★ Some stoppers may be embarrassed by chewing in public
★ It can be tricky if you have dentures
★ Your chewing technique must be right
★ Early side-effects might put you off

NICOTINE PATCHES

Nicotine patches were first introduced in the UK in 1992 and they've been available over the counter at pharmacies (and other stores in the US) since then. Patches come in three different strengths, 15 mg, 10 mg and 5 mg. Some are intended for use around the clock (24-hr patches) and others (16-hr patches) are for daytime use only. They all have the advantage that they deliver a steady dose of nicotine into the blood through your skin and are extremely easy to use. Many quitters have found that by using patches they can get through the critical first few days in a calmer frame of mind without cigarettes. Although they still experience cravings, these are more manageable as a result of wearing patches and they are able to get on with their lives quite well.

What to expect
When you put a nicotine patch on you won't detect much happening for a while as it takes time for nicotine to seep into your skin and build up in your bloodstream. The exact amount of time this takes depends on the patch in question. In the UK the Niquitin CQ 24-hour patch takes 4 hours to reach its peak level while the Nicotinell 24-hr patch takes about 6 but it needn't make all that much difference as you can put the patch on before you go to bed. Nicorette 16-hour patches and Boots own-brand take 8 hours to build up and then tail off towards bedtime. If you decide to go for these you could try setting your alarm an hour or so early, putting a patch on and then going back to sleep until it's starting to build up to helpful levels.

What to choose
If you are a regular, fairly dependent smoker (check your score by completing the DIY Nicotine Dependence Test on p. 46 if you haven't done so already) then you need to start with the highest dose patch. Wear it for a few weeks (preferably 8 but no less than 4) before switching to a lower strength. Lighter smokers could start with the middle-strength patch and wear that for the same amount of time.

Daytime only or 24-hr?

Some people get very worried about missing that first cigarette of the day and opt for the 24-hr patch so that when they wake up there will already be nicotine in their system to help with this. Others aren't so worried about the first one and manage very well with daytime-only patches. Some quitters find that wearing patches at night can give them vivid 'nicotine dreams', maybe because they're not used to having nicotine in their bloodstream all the time but your sleep may be a bit disturbed when you quit anyway so it's hard to be sure what causes this.

Sensitive skin?

If you have sensitive skin then you may get a bit of a reaction to whichever patch you choose. In most cases this is no more serious than a slight reddening and a bit of itchiness but it makes sense to vary the place where you stick the patch each day so as to give your skin a rest. You can put your patch on any dry, hair-free part of your body (although it's best to avoid your face!) and most people opt for the upper arms, shoulders or chest. The adhesive used to make the patches stick to you may leave marks on your skin and a good tip for removing these is to use a little acetone (nail varnish remover) on a bit of cotton wool.

PROS

★ Patches provide the right dose of nicotine automatically
★ Patches are very easy to use (you can just stick and go!)
★ 24-hr patches may help with anxieties about early morning cravings
★ It's highly unlikely that you'll get hooked on patches long-term

CONS

★ A few people may get a bad skin reaction when using patches

★ 24-hr patches may disturb your sleep
★ Wearing a patch won't satisfy the desire to put something in your mouth!

NICOTINE NASAL SPRAY (NNS)
FOR THOSE WHO NEED SOMETHING STRONGER …

The most powerful kind or NRT yet developed comes in the form of a nasal spray. At the moment you can only get it on private prescription in the UK and many people are still unaware that it is possible to get it at all. Not all pharmacies keep it in stock but it is possible to track it down if you try. The spray is recommended for heavier, more dependent smokers who've tried everything else and found that they really do need a lot of help to reduce their level of craving. It's probably not the first line treatment for light or even medium smokers but for those with a high level of dependence it can work very well.

How do you use it?
The spray comes in the form of a small bottle of nicotine solution with a nozzle at the top. What you have to do is tip your head back, insert the nozzle into your nozzle (sorry, nose!) and then push down on the top of the bottle. This will send a puff of spray up your nostril and one dose = one spray up each nostril. It's recommended that, to start with, you use 1 to 2 doses per hour and then after 8 weeks cut down by about half.

Fast and furious!
Nicotine nasal spray is not for the faint-hearted – it delivers a shot of nicotine very rapidly through the lining of the nose and can really help deal with cravings quickly, but have a tissue ready when you first start using it as it will probably make your eyes water. (I know because I've tried it.) It might also

make you sneeze to start with but just as with gum, the side-effects soon stop being a problem and after a day or so you'll get used to the spray.

Will I get hooked?

Nicotine Nasal Spray is the strongest and quickest method of getting nicotine short of smoking and thus it's also the most likely to cause dependence – but for heavy smokers it's still a much better bet than continuing to smoke and few people have had trouble coming off it anyway. If you've tried everything else (properly) and you still have terrible cravings for nicotine then it could be a wise choice. You'll need the help and support of your doctor who can monitor the amount you use and help you with the weaning off process when the time comes so talk it over with him or her if you're interested in giving it a go.

PROS
★ Highly effective craving relief
★ Fast-acting
★ Can help heavily addicted smokers

CONS
★ Causes nasal irritation at first
★ A bit embarrassing to use in company!
★ A bit more likely to cause dependence
★ It might be hard to get hold of in some areas

THE NICOTINE INHALER OR 'INHALATOR'

The 'Inhalator' is a relative newcomer to the array of NRT products currently available and it's about as strong as 2mg gum in terms of the amount of nicotine it delivers. It looks a bit like a cross between a pen and a cigarette holder and consists of a mouthpiece and a cartridge into which you insert a 10 mg nicotine 'plug'. To use the inhalator you simply suck on it and nicotine vapour mixed with menthol passes into your mouth and throat where it is absorbed into your body. The amount of nicotine you get depends to some extent on how much air you draw through the cartridge and on how high the air temperature is but one draw on it gives you about a tenth of the nicotine you'd get from a puff on a cigarette.

Why choose the Inhaler?

Some people really miss the sensation of putting something into their mouths when they stop smoking and perhaps the sensation of drawing in vapour as well. The Inhalator mimics the action of smoking to some extent so for those for whom this seems important it may be a good choice. The cartridge itself looks quite attractive although some might feel that the way it works is a little too similar to the action of smoking; it just depends how you look at it. If you're a light or medium smoker and you can't get on with patches or gum then it might be the right product for you, especially if you also miss that hand-to-mouth sensation.

PROS

★ Helps if you can't think what to do with your hands!
★ It's unlikely to cause dependence
★ It's fairly convenient to carry around
★ Allows you to regulate your own dose
★ Simulates the action of sucking on a cigarette
★ May help to prevent too much compensatory eating!

CONS

★ Not so good for more heavily dependent smokers
★ May attract attention when used in public
★ May be a bit too similar to the action of smoking and remind you of what you're missing

THE MICROTAB

The most recent addition to the NRT collection is the new Microtab. It works on the same principle as all other NRT products, i.e. it supplies a steady measured dose of nicotine to help reduce your cravings when you've stopped smoking. The difference with this product is that instead of chewing it like gum you allow it to dissolve slowly under your tongue (it takes about 20 to 30 minutes to dissolve completely). The nicotine is slowly absorbed through the lining of your mouth and will give about the same relief from cravings as you'd expect from 2mg gum.

The daily dose
How many Microtabs you use each day depends on how many cigarettes you currently smoke. If you're on about 20 cigarettes a day then you'll need to use one Microtab every hour but you can increase this to two per hour if you need more help with cravings. As a general rule of thumb follow the dosing instructions below:

If you smoke less than 20 cigs per day
USE 8 – 12 Microtabs per day

If you smoke more than 20 cigs per day
USE 16 – 24 Microtabs per day

Stick with it!
Don't be tempted to reduce your dose too early on or you might find that the cravings come back and you could easily relapse. You should ideally carry on using it for 3 months after stopping but do give it at least 8 weeks before gradually reducing your dose. As with all NRT products, the nicotine builds up gradually in your bloodstream with each dose you take so you must take them regularly and you must take enough or it won't work.

Safety first

So far, trials on the Microtab have shown that it has very few side-effects and that it is very safe to use. The likelihood is that you'll be taking in about a third of the nicotine you were getting from cigarettes so there's no danger of taking too much, provided you follow the instructions and the dosing guide above. If you were to swallow the tablets then the nicotine would pass into your stomach and wouldn't be absorbed which would be a complete waste of time and money.

Advantages over other forms of NRT?

The Microtab comes in a circular dispenser that looks quite attractive and is small enough to fit into your pocket or your handbag. The Microtabs themselves are pretty small, about the size of a beverage sweetener and fit comfortably under the tongue so people won't know that you're using it unless you want them to.

PROS

★ It's easy to adjust your dose
★ Discreet to use
★ Few side-effects

CONS

★ You might not use enough for maximum benefit

COMBINATIONS OF NRT THERAPIES

The one thing we haven't yet covered is the possible benefit of using more than one NRT product at the same time. Researchers are investigating whether this might be a good strategy for some quitters but as yet there is no clear advice. Trials of patches and the spray, or patches and gum, would seem to indicate that having 'background' help from a patch and the 'emergency' option of a quick craving-buster like the spray does improve success rates. It certainly seems logical that this kind of combination could give extra help and might overcome the most common problem of people using too little NRT. The day is probably coming when NRT products will be licensed for use in combination with one another and maybe even with other treatments. Some clinicians are already recommending that their patients try this kind of approach and if you decide to give it a go then you may find stopping easier as a result. It's as well to consult your doctor if you have any concerns about it but bear in mind that by far the biggest risk is continuing to smoke.

ZYBAN (BUPROPION)

The search for new non-nicotine treatments for smokers continues and a surprising development has recently emerged from the United States. Zyban (also known as Bupropion) is the first non-nicotine prescription medicine for use in stopping smoking and it is being marketed in the States by Glaxo-Wellcome. Originally used as an anti-depressant (under the name 'Wellbutrin') Zyban was found to double people's chances of success compared with a placebo (dummy treatment) in a study carried out at the Mayo Nicotine Dependence Center, and other studies have shown similar results. Although research is ongoing these early studies have indicated that Zyban may be even more effective than NRT and can be used alongside nicotine treatments to improve success rates.

How does it work?
Zyban is thought to work on the nervous system to counteract the symptoms of withdrawal (e.g. irritability and dizziness) but it also seems to work at a more fundamental level by reducing the urge to smoke, possibly by interfering with the chemical pathways of nicotine addiction in the brain. We still don't fully understand exactly how Zyban helps people to stop

smoking. Previous experiments with anti-depressant drugs haven't produced good results but the effects of Zyban are fairly dramatic in research terms so it's clearly not a development to be ignored. It is currently proving popular with quitters in the States where more than 3 million prescriptions for it have been issued since it was first brought onto the market.

The treatment plan

Interestingly, people start taking Zyban before they stop smoking and then set a quit date 8 to 14 days after their first dose of the drug. This is usually done with the help and support of a health professional and when the Quit Day arrives the doses of Zyban continue but all smoking stops. By this time the body has become accustomed to the presence of the drug which should have built up to the required levels and started to reduce the person's desire to smoke, making it easier for them to stay smoke-free after the Quit Day. Most patients are then advised to keep taking Zyban for 7 to 12 weeks to help them achieve long-term success.

Side-effects

The most common side-effects associated with the use of Zyban are: weight-loss, insomnia and nervousness. Occasionally people may also experience: constipation, a dry mouth, headaches, nausea and excessive sweating. In very rare cases the drug can cause seizures (fits) but it's important to put the risks in perspective. The 3 million prescriptions issued so far in the States haven't caused any more seizures than you'd normally expect to get in a population of that size so it's not really something to cause too much alarm. Not everyone gets side-effects and in those who do they are usually quite mild.

Who should *not* take Zyban?

Zyban isn't recommended for pregnant women or those who are breast-feeding. It's also not suitable for people with eating disorders or anyone with an increased risk of seizures (those with a history of fits or who have suffered brain damage). As with any medication it's wise to consult your doctor before starting treatment.

Availability

At the time of writing Zyban is not yet available to quitters in the UK but Glaxo-Wellcome have applied for permission to market it in the European Union so it may soon be available.

GLUCOSE – THE SWEET TREATMENT

Although research is still at an early stage, there is some evidence that eating glucose tablets when you feel a craving and at regular intervals during the day may help you stop smoking. The theory is the brainchild of Professor Robert West, an internationally renowned researcher into the process of stopping smoking, and I was involved in one of the first clinical trials of this new approach to treating smokers.

Why glucose?

The rationale behind using glucose is twofold: Firstly, it may well be that over the countless years that many of us smoke, we lose the ability to distinguish properly between hunger cravings and nicotine cravings. When we eat it usually takes away our desire for nicotine (albeit temporarily) and when we smoke it tends to suppress our appetite for food, so the two are closely related in our minds. So, when we stop smoking, we are attacked by both types of craving at once and interpret both as a desperate need for a smoke. The other way that glucose may help is by stimulating the production of serotonin in the brain. Serotonin is known as a 'feel good' chemical and is thought to put us in a better mood. If you feel happier then you're less likely to crack up, so glucose may help smokers in this way too.

Blood sugar levels

Eating regular meals and starting the day with a healthy breakfast helps to keep our blood sugar and energy levels nice and
steady, but many smokers are irregular eaters and they often
skip breakfast (usually in favour of a few cigarettes!). As a
result they suffer from big dips in blood sugar and strong cravings for food that may 'join forces' with their cravings for nicotine. It's hard to resist those cravings if you're physically weak
and in need of food but if you eat glucose tablets at intervals
through the day, your blood sugar levels will stay higher and
you should feel better able to cope. Studies have shown that it
can reduce craving in the short-term and new research will
test whether it also helps in the long run. The jury is still out,
so to speak, but unless you're a diabetic, eating glucose tablets
can't do you any harm so I'd recommend using them in addition to NRT for maximum help with cravings.

OTHER NON-NICOTINE PRODUCTS

Apart from Zyban and glucose there are a number of non-nicotine products which are marketed as aids to stopping smoking.
Unfortunately none of them have any firm evidence of effectiveness and unscrupulous manufacturers continue to make
money out of desperate smokers who believe the promises on
the packaging.

Herbal Capsules (Nicobrevin)

This product is unlikely to help you stop smoking. It's
intended to improve your respiratory abilities and control
withdrawal symptoms but there's no good evidence to show
that it does anything helpful for smokers either in the short-or
long-term. Herbs sound nice and natural and the manufacturers promote the fact that their product contains no nicotine,
further contributing to the myth that nicotine is the most dangerous constituent in tobacco smoke. All in all, I'd say don't
waste your money on it.

Silver Acetate Gum & Mouthwash (Giv-Up)
The idea behind these products is that after using them cigarettes will taste unpleasant. Again there's no evidence that they work and of course you only get the effect when you actually light up, which kind of defeats the object of the exercise! They also give some people indigestion and nausea so I'd say give them a wide berth.

Dummy Cigarettes (Flowers, Crave-away, Everlasting Cigarettes)
These plastic replicas of cigarettes are supposed to simulate the hand-to-mouth feel of a real cigarette and give you something to fiddle with when you crave a smoke. There's no evidence that they help and they may even trigger cravings by reminding you of the very thing you're trying to do without. If you want to buy one as part of your overall armoury of things to use in an emergency then by all means do but make sure you have some products that really do work as well!

Herbal Cigarettes
I believe that a great many would-be stoppers try herbal cigarettes once but that most don't go back for more because smoking them is rather like inhaling the smoke from a burning compost heap without the pay-off of any nicotine. The idea behind them is that they allow you to smoke without giving you any nicotine, which is crazy for two reasons:

1. Even though herbal cigarettes don't contain nicotine, smoking them will hurt you by putting tar and carbon monoxide into your body

2. Even if you do manage to persist with them (and they really are pretty revolting in my opinion) you'll still be hooked on the whole idea of smoking something and they'll probably make you miss your nicotine 'hit' all the more

The other point to note about some herbal cigarettes is that they smell very similar to cannabis/marijuana so you might find that people follow you around at parties or give you funny looks on the bus!

Graduated filters

These products are designed to fit over the end of your cigarette and filter out some of the tar and nicotine that passes into your body. Different filters filter out more and more over a few weeks until (in theory) you become accustomed to lower levels of nicotine, and so find stopping completely more manageable.

Much depends on how you use these filters and for how long. They may help you prepare to quit by reducing your nicotine dependence but only if you use them every time you smoke and don't up your tobacco consumption to supplement your nicotine intake. Your best option is to stop smoking completely so don't be beguiled by the idea that using filters will enable you to carry on smoking 'safely'. If you want to use them in the days and weeks immediately before stopping then follow the instructions faithfully and don't put off stopping completely in favour of continuing to smoke with filters.

Tobacco-flavoured chewing gum

Chewing this type of gum when you have a craving won't do you any harm, but there's no evidence that it'll help either. Chewing can be a useful distraction tactic but you might as well use nicotine gum for help with cravings or regular gum if you just want something to do with your mouth and a pleasant taste.

Scented inhalers (Logado)

These scented herb-based inhalers are meant to be sniffed when you have a craving and in some way help with withdrawal but as one of my patients once remarked, 'it just made my handbag smell funny'. Carry one around if you wish, but don't expect it to help with cravings much.

A Summary of Drug Treatments That Work

This table details all the drug therapies that are currently available in the US and the UK together with their brand names and manufacturers. The names tend to be quite similar and as the list of products grows it can all get a bit confusing so refer to this list if you want to know who makes what and where.

PRODUCT	NAME & UK MANUFACTURER	NAME & US MANUFACTURER
Gum	Nicorette (P&U)	Nicorette (SB)
		Nicotrol (McNeill)
Patches	NiQuitin CQ (SB)	Nicoderm CQ (SB)
	Nicotinell (Nov)	Nicotrol (McNeill)
	Nicorette (P&U)	Habitrol (Nov)
	Boots Own-Brand (P&U/Boots)	Prostep (Elan)
Nicorette Nasal Spray	Nicorette (P&U)	Nicotrol NS (McNeill)
Inhalator (Inhaler)	Nicorette Inhalator (P&U)	Nicotrol (McNeill)
Zyban (non-nicotine product)	Not currently available (licence pending)	Zyban (Glaxo)

KEY TO MANUFACTURERS

P&U	Pharmacia & Upjohn
SB	SmithKline Beecham
Nov	Novartis Consumer Healthcare
McNeill	McNeill Pharmaceuticals
Glaxo	Glaxo Wellcome
Elan	Elan Pharma
Boots	Boots the Chemist

GROUP THERAPY

Group counselling courses for people who want to stop smoking can really help some but their availability is pretty patchy at the moment. Groups are relatively cheap to run and are popular with those who enjoy the social support of a collection of others who are 'all in the same boat'. Courses vary as to structure and content but a great many have been run as part of the ongoing research into new treatments for smokers. From this research, a basic pattern of group treatment has emerged which seems, in most cases, to produce reasonable results.

Course structure
Some of the clinics offering these courses are based in Health Promotion Units, whilst others are run from hospitals or specialised research institutions. The level of staffing and the amount of time and money that can be spent on recruiting and assessing individual group members varies, but it's common for 'patients' to be referred to such services by doctors and other health professionals in the area. Large numbers of recruits are needed to produce groups of a good size, so it's also common practice for adverts to be placed in local newspapers so that people can apply to join the course without needing to visit their doctors. Courses usually consist of 4 to 8 sessions (6 is probably about right) each lasting about an hour. Further down the track, successful quitters may be followed up to check how they are getting on. This is often done at 3, 6 or 12 months (and sometimes at all 3 points); the Quit Day usually falls on the first session (if group members have been briefed and assessed in advance) or on the second session. My own preference was for the latter with session one being an 'introductory session' in which members could get to know one another and prepare for the Quit Day armed with the right information.

Strength in numbers

Even in the most determined groups, many people will relapse. (A good success rate at 12 months from Quit day would be around 25% of those who started the course. It's important, therefore, that a group course should start out with a decent number of members – 15 to 25 is about right, depending on the size of the room available. If you start with 20 people, then even after a few have fallen by the wayside, you've still got a decent sized group and members will continue to feel positive about the course. If, on the other hand, you start off with only 6 or 7 people, then by the time you get halfway through and a few have disappeared, those that remain start to feel like a dwindling band of doomed quitters and morale dips significantly. The success of the group depends partly on the skill and experience of the therapist running the course, but group members can give one another valuable support as the course progresses and they pass through the withdrawal process together.

CO monitoring

Before the course begins, it's common for smokers to have their carbon monoxide levels checked and their level of nicotine dependence assessed (in much the same way as you checked yours in the DIY Dependence Test earlier in this book). Armed with this information, the therapist can then advise them on suitable treatments and potential problems. CO monitoring also has enormous value as a means of motivating people because it only takes a couple of days for readings to fall to those of a non-smoker once you stop. On the first week of a counselling course, smokers hardly dare to look at the digital read-out on the machine, and are often deeply concerned by the fact that their readings are higher (sometimes by a wide margin) than those of non-smokers (non-smokers usually score less than 10). By contrast, when quitters return to the group after a week of non-smoking, they can't wait to get their hands on a CO Monitor and see the change! It gives them a very real psychological boost at a crucial stage of quitting and provides a much needed 'window' as to what is going on inside the body of a recovering ex-smoker.

The first encounter

When the group first gets together for a session, it's important that the members get to know one another and focus on their real reasons for stopping. The therapist may get each person to say a bit about themselves and their individual reasons, before advising the whole group about the best ways to avoid relapse and deal with withdrawal. The course structure will also be explained so that everyone knows what to expect and people are given an opportunity to voice their concerns or worries about stopping.

Commitment

At the Quit session itself, some therapists encourage people to stand up and make a formal commitment to quitting to the group. Members of the group throw away any cigarettes that they have left and publicly declare their intention not to smoke again after the session. This might sound a bit theatrical or 'staged' but hearing yourself say the words, and the simple act of making a commitment to the group can be very powerful. A strong sense of 'not wanting to let everyone down' keeps many quitters on the straight and narrow when they might otherwise have relapsed.

Place your bets!

Another tactic used in some groups requires that you actually make a financial commitment to stopping for good. Group members may be asked to 'buddy up' with a partner and then both give the therapist an amount of money for safekeeping. If *either* of them cracks up then *both* forfeit their cash, and this acts as another incentive when things get tough. This model is favoured by Dr Peter Hajek at the Royal London Hospital and although it struck me as a bit 'whacky' to start with, it does seem to get results. The amounts of money aren't large in most cases, just as much as the individual wants to commit, and 'forfeited' money doesn't go into the therapist's pocket – it's usually used to finance an end of course celebration ...

Session content

As the counselling course progresses, members report their highs and lows and discuss issues that are important to them. These typically include weight-gain, cravings, how to cope with withdrawal and the physical improvement they've noticed since stopping. Group members who've relapsed are usually encouraged to come back and explain how they tripped up but many of those who relapse just stop attending, perhaps because they feel that they've let others down and aren't ready to have another go. At the end of the course, those who've been successful are usually over the worst of withdrawal and are very pleased to be non-smokers. At this point the therapist will probably focus on ways to prevent relapse in the weeks and months after the course finishes and make arrangements for people to follow up at a later stage. After 6 weeks of hard work and mutual support, group members are often very close and some worry that they may not be able to cope without the weekly meetings but most are ready to take the next step. They have managed to cope with a great many situations without smoking by this time and have more confidence in their own ability to stay smoke-free.

Fun!

I've run many group courses in the past and while the character of each group varies, most are great fun. Sharing people's experiences as they pass through an important, life-changing event like giving up smoking can be very moving at times and hilarious at others. Here's how one lively ex-smoker felt about her experiences in group counselling:

> 'When I finally got up the nerve to look around for some
> help in quitting, I wasn't sure I could do it on my own.
> Luckily my local Health Promotion Unit was running a
> counselling course for people who wanted to quit and I
> managed to get into a group. I wasn't sure how I'd cope
> with a bunch of strangers but in fact it was brilliant to be
> with people who really understood and I thoroughly
> enjoyed it! We had a really good laugh each week
> and it helped a lot to be able to go in there and say
> "I want to go and smash a plate!" and have everyone
> saying, Yes! I know exactly what you mean!'

Groups are perfect for outgoing, sociable people who like getting together with others, so if you fall into this category and there is a group service for smokers near you, I'd advise you to check it out. If, however, there is some reason why you can't or don't want to attend a group, then there's no reason why you can't be equally successful at home.

Aversion therapy

Many a smoker will relate tales of how an irate parent discovered them puffing and then forced them to smoke in order to make them sick put them off the whole thing (see Dave Allen's case study for a classic example of this backfiring on an unsuspecting parent). Aversion therapy involves pairing the experience of doing something (in this case smoking) with some highly unpleasant experience like nausea in order to 'extinguish' the undesirable behaviour. Unfortunately it only seems to work very rarely as a deterrent and because it is so unpleasant it never really caught on. Back in the 1970s there were a number of 'rapid smoking' type variations on this basic theme.

Some involved smoking until you were sick while others advocated sniffing jam-jars full of dog-ends. If you want to try any of these activities before stopping then good luck to you but as a treatment it's not really to be recommended and rapid smoking is definitely a bad idea for pregnant smokers or those with any kind of smoking-related disease.

Hypnotherapy – mumbo-jumbo or miracle cure?

When we think of hypnosis we tend to think of it either as part of a one-to-one therapeutic process, or as entertainment. It is used to heal and it is used to make us laugh – and who wouldn't laugh at otherwise normal people behaving like chickens, or Martians, or Elvis? Possibly their families, but for the rest of us there is no pleasure to match that of somebody else making a fool of themselves.

Yet in other parts of the world, and at different times, holy men such as yogis, priests and dervishes have used all manner of techniques to help alter consciousness for different ends. Chanting, drumming and dancing have all been used, and references to what we now call hypnosis can be found in the writings of many religions including the Bible and the Talmud.

In the West, scientists and medics have explored the process of altering consciousness for the purpose of healing since the late eighteenth century, when Dr. Franz Mesmer developed healing by what he called 'animal magnetism'. You won't be surprised to learn that this process became known as 'mesmerism'. In the nineteenth century interest in the subject grew, and physician James Braid renamed the process 'hypnosis' (derived from the Greek word for sleep – hypnos). A British surgeon in India, James Esdail, apparently performed 2,000 operations using only hypnosis as an anaesthetic, with patients allegedly feeling no pain! Towards the end of the century the British Medical Association (BMA) reported favourably on the use of hypnosis, and it was widely used during the First World War.

Hypnotism enters the mainstream

The late twentieth century has seen the founding of a number of organisations promoting hypnotherapy, offering training and monitoring its use in a range of medical applications. In 1968 the British Society of Medical and Dental Hypnosis was founded, and in 1973 the Hypnotherapy Register was set up. This was administered by the National Council for Psychotherapists, which was later to become the National Council for Hypnotherapy.

Famous fans of hypnosis

Hypnosis now has an undisputed place in the mainstream of modern medicine, and has been used by a string of famous people. Kevin Costner is reputed to have used a hypnotist to cure his seasickness during the making of *Waterworld*, and the composer Rachmaninov is said to have written a concerto following a suggestion made to him whilst under hypnosis. Perhaps the most famous hypnotist in the UK, Paul McKenna has worked with sportsmen such as Frank Bruno, Nigel Benn and the Crystal Palace football team and his TV show attracts huge audiences.

How does hypnosis work?

Hypnosis is perhaps best understood as a relaxed state in which the mind ceases to be concerned with the everyday. In such a state the subconscious part of the mind is particularly responsive to suggestion, which can be especially useful if the conscious mind is erecting obstacles to changes of behaviour. Thoughts such as 'I'll never be able to stop smoking' are very powerful, and hypnosis seeks to tackle them by making equally strong counter-suggestions.

Can anyone be hypnotised?

Everybody is different. The more 'suggestible' you are and the more you go along with the process the more likely it is that you will respond to hypnosis. We all vary in this respect, some people are very easy to hypnotise (such as those you see on TV shows) whereas others have a very low 'suggestibility rating' and are unlikely to enter a deep trance state no matter how hard the hypnotist tries. It's worth bearing in mind that it takes long and careful searching to find the right people to take part in hypnotism stage shows. Hundreds may be auditioned for a show and the people who get picked are chosen not only because they can slip quickly into a deeply hypnotic state, but for a general ability to respond to suggestion in an extrovert and amusing way. It is definitely not the case that everyone has a comedy turn inside them just waiting to be freed by hypnotism, or that they will automatically start behaving in embarrassing ways at the drop of a hat!

Is hypnotism safe?

In most applications hypnotism has no known side-effects – any reported problems have been through its misuse. However, there are some people for whom hypnotism can be dangerous, notably those suffering from epilepsy, psychosis, schizophrenia and other mental health disorders.

Hypnotism and stopping smoking

In recent years, many claims have been made for hypnotism as an effective aid to stopping smoking and smokers wanting help with quitting now form a sizeable proportion of those taking to the hypnotherapist's couch. The theory is that the therapist acts on underlying impulses to weaken the desire to smoke, or to strengthen the desire to stop.

What usually happens

Once you have been hypnotised, the therapist will make suggestions for you to act upon after you are brought out of your hypnotic state. There are many approaches but one of the most common is based on the 'one session, three point' method. The patient is told that:

    i)   tobacco smoke is poison
    ii) the patient is entitled to protection from smoke
    iii) there are advantages to not smoking

Some approaches also include training in self-hypnosis, which can be used at will by the patient.

How much does it cost?

You can expect to pay between £20 and £30 per one-hour session in the UK, although I've heard of people charging up to £60 per hour so be on your guard. Avoid any therapist asking you to make a big payment 'up front' – if you don't feel comfortable with the treatment it is harder to walk away.

Will hypnotherapy help you to quit?

This, of course is the $64,000 question and for a number of reasons there isn't a clear answer yet. For one thing it's jolly hard to carry out reliable research because of differences between smokers (those suggestibility ratings again) and differences between therapists who tend to have different treatment styles and levels of skill. Hypnotherapy has been quite successful in treating other disorders such as chronic pain and asthma but studies of the results for smokers are inconclusive. The main problem is that many therapists don't calculate their success rates in the recommended way, so the results they claim to achieve may be misleading. The view of the highly respected Cochrane Research Group, which recently reviewed all the available research on this subject, is that at the moment there is 'insufficient evidence to recommend hypnotherapy as a specific treatment for smoking cessation'.

Many have found hypnotherapy useful in a range of ways, and I welcome any product or technique that will help people quit smoking but at the moment there really isn't much evidence to suggest that hypnosis can help you to stop. More research is needed but in the meantime you might be better off using therapies for which there is good evidence of effectiveness e.g. Nicotine Replacement. If you want to try hypnosis as well then it's unlikely to do you any harm; it might even strengthen your resolve but it's probably unwise to regard it as a 'magic' solution that will make stopping effortless after just one session.

ACUPUNCTURE – IS THERE ANY POINT FOR SMOKERS?

Acupuncture has been used to treat nicotine dependence in the West since 1973 when some opium smokers in Hong Kong were given 'electroacupuncture' for pain relief and claimed that it made their withdrawal symptoms less severe. Early research studies suggested that acupuncture might also help to reduce the severity of nicotine withdrawal and some remarkably high success rates were claimed.

What happens?
Fine needles are usually inserted in points on the ear, face and body (usually for about 20 minutes) and sometimes an electrical current is passed through them (this is what is known as 'electroacupuncture'). Occasionally the needles are held in place with surgical tape for several days; this procedure is called 'indwelling' acupuncture.

The story so far ...
Some therapists believe that the insertion of needles may trigger the release of endorphins (the body's own natural painkillers) and so make people feel better. The trouble is that most of the studies that have so far been carried out to investigate whether acupuncture really helps smokers weren't properly controlled or 'randomised' (i.e. they didn't compare the treatment with other therapies correctly and weren't scientific enough to be reliable). Most also failed to follow the volunteers up for a long-enough period to check whether they

managed to stay smoke-free after the treatment. A recent review of all the research conducted on this subject revealed that, as yet, there's no good evidence to suggest that acupuncture helps people to stop smoking. It may have a slight effect in the short-term and so be marginally better than doing nothing at all but if you're going to quit you'd be much better advised to try one of the treatments that clearly does work.

The mysterious East

Acupuncture and other forms of eastern medicine continue to excite interest in Western societies, perhaps because they are so ancient and mysterious. Disillusionment with modern scientific drug therapies may lead people to experiment with all manner of 'alternative remedies'. The last thing I want to do is pour cold water on people's hopes of a breakthrough but it's as well to be practical and maintain a sense of perspective on a subject as important as quitting smoking. Don't dismiss therapies that do work in favour of those that are as yet unproven and don't (for heaven's sake!) hand over large amounts of money for 'trendy' new-age therapies that seem to promise the earth. If there is a great new discovery that helps smokers, I'll be happy to welcome it from any quarter or medical tradition, but until then let's stick to the facts.

BEFORE YOU MAKE YOUR CHOICE ...

Stop-smoking programmes and treatments often quote success rates of 80% or 90% but how are these rates calculated? Can you really trust them? How many people really do succeed and for how long?

Asking the right questions

Giving up smoking successfully could save your life and we believe that you deserve the best information about your chances of success with any product or treatment. If you're considering trying a treatment or service to help you stop smoking then don't rely on percentages alone. By asking the questions that follow you'll get a much clearer idea of what your chances are and whether it's worth investing time, money and precious motivation on a particular product.

1. **Check** what kind of 'follow-up period' was used to calculate the success rates being claimed.

    Lots of people relapse when it comes to giving up smoking and it's quite normal to slip up before you get it right and stay off for good. Most relapsers do so fairly early on in the process, probably before the three-month mark so it's vital to ask when the success rates were calculated. In good quality research trials success rates are based on how many people are still smoke-free at 12 months from the time of treatment and you should look for rates based on a follow-up period of at least 6 months.

2. **Ask how** the clinic or therapist checks whether people are smoke-free. Sadly it's not enough to ask people whether they're still not smoking. You have to check it physically to get an accurate picture. It's not that everyone lies but people might say what they think the therapist wants to hear or they might feel too mixed up to admit that 'they've fallen off the wagon'. Researchers usually test results by giving people a carbon monoxide breath test which can show if they've smoked in the past 24 hours. This is the minimum level of testing that you should look for and in some research programmes it's also backed up by blood and saliva tests.

3. **Find out** how many people they based their results on. For a set of success rates to have any real meaning they must have been drawn from the results of a reasonably large number of people or they are unlikely to hold good

for the majority of quitters. If one person manages to stop after using a product then the maker could claim a 100% success rate but this wouldn't really tell you anything except that it worked for that particular individual.

4. **Enquire** about the 'ones that got away'! When researchers try to contact people to follow them up it's inevitable that in some cases they've moved or can't be reached. It's not possible to say whether they've succeeded or not so, to be on the safe side, it's assumed that they've relapsed. Some Quit Programmes may offer a money-back guarantee or repeat treatment to relapsers and then, if people don't return, count them as successes. That's how they come up with sky-high rates like 80% after just one treatment! Some of their customers may have stayed away because they've cracked it, but others may well have relapsed and decided not to come back for any number of other reasons.

What sort of success rates are realistic?
There's been an enormous amount of research done on what helps smokers to stop and the best, properly evaluated programmes can sometimes achieve success rates of up to 35% if they give people Nicotine Replacement Therapy, intensive counselling support and long-term follow-up. This compares well with the 'self-quit rate' (the success rates you get if people get no help at all) which is normally about 1% or 2% – but if you see adverts for rates above 40% then beware! Ask questions and find out how they came up with the figures before you sign up or part with any money.

A few words about willpower
We've all heard of the 'Willpower Method' of stopping smoking. Those who relapse often blame their lack of willpower for their problems, but is it really true that some of us have

barrow-loads of the stuff, while others were 'behind the door' when it was handed out? Worries about how much willpower they have trouble a great many smokers as their chosen Quit Day gets closer:

> *'I really do want to stop smoking more than anything,*
> *but I'm not sure if I've got enough willpower'*

Many quitters see "willpower" as one of the most important factors in the success or failure of their efforts to stop smoking and doubts about willpower may prevent them from really committing themselves to a quit attempt. These doubts can even stop them from admitting to themselves and others that they really do want to quit.

So, what is willpower?

Researcher and clinical psychologist Dr Jonathan Foulds has suggested that the concept of willpower involves two main elements: strength and consistency of purpose over a period of time. These are particularly important when the going gets tough. This means having the strength of will to say, 'no' to smoking even when you have other pressures in your life and even when someone is tempting you by waving a packet of cigarettes right under your nose.

WILLPOWER = STRENGTH OF PURPOSE + CONSISTENCY

Negative thinking

People who want to stop smoking but doubt that they have enough willpower can fall into a pattern of negative thinking that is unhelpful. They want to succeed all right, but previous relapses and past disappointments may have all but convinced them that they haven't got what it takes. This negative frame of mind and lack of confidence may well prejudice their chances of success. They need to understand why they've

relapsed in the past and learn to build up their willpower
reserves for the task ahead.

How long can you hold your breath?

While it's certainly true that some people are better at sticking
to their decisions than others, I haven't seen much evidence to
show that this relates in any meaningful way to success in
stopping smoking. However, some work has been done to
investigate whether people who succeed in this are also better
at doing other difficult things or putting up with discomforts of
some sort. One such study was carried out by Dr Peter Hajek
of the University of London: Peter reasoned that people who
succeed in stopping smoking may be better at putting up with
physical discomfort than those who don't. He and his colleagues tested this by asking a large number of people (who
were attending a smokers' clinic) to take a deep breath and
hold it for as long as possible. Holding your breath for more
than a few moments involves putting up with a certain level of
discomfort, so it was one way to separate the 'sheep from the
goats' so to speak. Some people had to let their breath go as
soon as they felt the need for some air, whereas others were
able to hold on a bit longer. The study found that, even after
excluding people with pre-existing breathing difficulties, those
who were able to hold their breath longest were also more
likely to succeed in stopping smoking.

Zero tolerance

It seems, then, that in order to succeed in stopping smoking
you have to be ready to put up with a certain level of discomfort for a while. You also have to make the decision that no
amount of discomfort is a sufficient excuse for having a smoke.
Once you've made that decision quite clearly in your own
mind, it can actually make things easier. Some people are constantly plagued by thoughts like, 'If I get one more bit of bad

news then I'll be so stressed I'll have to smoke' or 'If one more person offers me a cigarette then the craving will be too much and I'll have to have one'. But if you make the decision that 'No stress or temptation will be sufficient reason for me to smoke', you won't have to keep weighing up whether or not your stress or craving are enough to allow you to have one.

The power of symbolism

One of the most important effects of people believing that they lack willpower is that this self-doubt may stop them from taking positive steps towards quitting. One example is the decision of whether or not to tell your friends and colleagues that you are stopping smoking. People who doubt their willpower are less likely to publicise their quit attempt, usually for fear of ridicule if they relapse. But it could be that the very act of telling people of your goal might encourage them to give you some helpful social support. At the very least it's likely to put some useful social pressure on you to remain smoke-free. There are a whole series of symbolic gestures you can make which will demonstrate the strength of your intention to stop smoking and help to build up your sense of your own willpower. Here are some suggestions:

(a) Throw out all your tobacco, lighters, ash-trays etc.
(b) Mark on a calendar each day free from tobacco
(c) Save all the money you would have spent on tobacco in a direct and visible way (e.g. putting it in an empty glass jar)
(d) Tell friends and colleagues about the quit attempt
(e) Read a book or magazine about stopping smoking!

Actions speak louder

Some of these actions will help you in directly practical ways (e.g. if there's no tobacco in the house it'll be harder for you to relapse at home) but I believe that they are also of symbolic value. They help to boost and maintain your 'willpower'. By taking these kinds of actions you'll be demonstrating to yourself that you really do mean business this time.

Assuming that you have already taken some steps to build up your willpower, the two additional pieces of advice I'd suggest are:

1. Don't waste it

Putting yourself in 'tempting' or stressful situations will mean that you have to use precious willpower to remain abstinent. I'd recommend avoiding these situations as far as possible, particularly during the first month of your quit attempt. On the positive side, using proven aids (such as Nicotine Replacement Therapy) to reduce withdrawal symptoms and craving may help to reduce the number of demands on your willpower reserves.

2. Use it when it really counts

Advance planning can enable you to build up and focus your willpower on the times when you know you will really need it. In order to do this you need to be able to identify and anticipate 'high-risk' situations such as a trip to the pub or an office party. Once you've identified a potentially risky situation you should take a little time beforehand to boost your willpower. Let's look at an example of how to do this. Suppose that tomorrow you have to attend the funeral of a close friend. This will almost certainly be a high-risk situation because it's bound to make you feel sad and emotional. Other people may well offer you cigarettes in order to be sociable and the seriousness of the occasion may make your attempt to stop smoking seem trivial (which it isn't):

Be prepared

Just before you go to the funeral you'll need to take a little time to remind yourself of the reasons why you've stopped smoking. Prepare a polite response to offers of cigarettes and remind yourself that it would be a great achievement to return from the funeral without having smoked. It may even be helpful to use 'mental visualisations' of yourself successfully avoiding smoking.

Willpower grows with success

It's sometimes said that money attracts money and that success breeds success. Well, in this case, the more smoke-free days you can successfully notch up on the calendar, the more your willpower should strengthen. Each time you negotiate your way through (or around) a risky situation your belief in your ability will grow. Most stoppers feel anxious and unsure on Day One, but those who win through to the 3-week point or further usually have much more confidence in their ability to resist temptation and manage their cravings effectively.

TEN TIPS TO HELP *YOU*
MAXIMISE YOUR WILLPOWER

1. Remind yourself of all your reasons for stopping smoking. Write them down and have a look at them when you feel at risk

2. Try to adopt the attitude that no amount of bad mood, stress or craving will be a sufficient excuse to smoke

3. Enlist the help of friends and colleagues to provide support and encouragement during the difficult times

4. Boost your self-confidence by reminding yourself of other difficult challenges in which you have successfully shown determination and willpower in the past

5. Visualise yourself coping successfully with 'high relapse risk' situations

6. Engage in symbolic activities which demonstrate your commitment to stopping smoking e.g. throwing tobacco in the bin, marking smoke-free days on the calendar, reading self-help literature etc.

7. Conserve your willpower by avoiding high-risk situations whenever possible and using NRT to reduce withdrawal and craving

8. Anticipate unavoidable 'high-risk' situations and build up your willpower beforehand

9. Keep a 'Stopping Diary' and record your achievements as you go along, e.g. 'Managed to visit bar without relapsing', 'Finished first day at work without smoking'

10. Write down the quit tips that have helped you so far, e.g. keeping busy, using patches etc.

CHAPTER 6

The Nicotine Withdrawal Syndrome

FEAR OF THE UNKNOWN

Most regular smokers will have smoked every day for a period of many years so the prospect of doing without tobacco and going through what is known as the 'Nicotine Withdrawal Syndrome' may seem very daunting. It's a bit like preparing to jump off a cliff or go for a moonwalk for most of us because we're not sure what to expect and we fear the unknown.

What can you expect?
Although it's not possible to be absolutely precise about the symptoms that each smoker will experience, a great deal of research has been done on this subject. We can now describe what a typical smoker is likely to go through after stopping and it's a great help knowing roughly what to expect and that others will have felt the same way. In this section I'm going to describe the various symptoms that are part of the process, how long they usually last and why they occur (if science has been able to give us a reason thus far). A word of caution though – individuals differ as to how many of these symptoms they get and to what degree. Don't be like the medical student who reads a book on tropical medicine and then decides that he has all manner of rare and ghastly diseases when in fact he is perfectly healthy ... You may well get some of the symptoms

I shall describe but there's no rule that says you have to have them all very badly!

Getting it in perspective

We know that certain symptoms are a part of the Nicotine Withdrawal Syndrome because:

(a) they appear when a person suddenly stops taking in nicotine or reduces the amount they take

(b) they get better or go away when you give the person some more nicotine (e.g. in the form of nicotine patches)

The main withdrawal symptoms that most people experience to some degree are: irritability, restlessness, depression, anxiety, difficulty concentrating, sleep disruption, hunger and craving for tobacco. It's important to remember before we go on to look at each of these in more detail, that they are all **temporary** and that none of them are life-threatening, unlike continuing to smoke! As well as explaining what the symptom is and how long it's likely to last, I'll also suggest some ways to cope with it when it arises so that you won't feel powerless to do anything about it. How you react can make a big difference and quite often there are practical ways to cut down the severity of withdrawal.

Irritability

'How dare you suggest that I'm irritable!'

About half of all quitters get irritable and snappy when they stop smoking and this is often at its worst in the first few days. Although it's a nuisance and may strain the patience of your nearest and dearest, it usually goes away within 3 to 4 weeks at which point your moods get more or less back to normal. Exactly why we feel irritable after stopping isn't clear but it's an anxious time and the unfamiliarity of the situation may be part of the cause. We don't feel as much in control as normal and so we lash out at those around us.

SO WHAT CAN YOU DO?

1. Sound the alarm!

The first thing to do is to warn friends, family and work-mates that your moods may be a bit unpredictable for 3 or 4 weeks. If you've tried to stop before and irritability has been a problem then there's all the more reason to do this. People who love you will probably be quite supportive even if you do lose your rag once too often and if you do end up getting a few people off side it really isn't the end of the world.

2. Avoid conflict situations

If a row does erupt, whether it's your fault or someone else's, your best bet is to walk away from it before things get too heated. Leave the room, the house, your desk or wherever the argument is taking place. Get outside for a burst of fresh air if possible and take some deep breaths to calm yourself down. Most rows start over something pretty trivial if we're honest and it's unlikely that the fate of the nation rests on the outcome so if you can't escape from the person you're arguing with try agreeing with them. It doesn't matter if deep down you don't mean it. Agreeing with their point of view or saying 'OK, we'll do things your way' will take the steam out of the argument. It'll be hard for them to carry on fighting if you back off and things will cool down quicker.

Restlessness

You may find that you just don't quite know what to do with yourself when you quit. You mooch about like a lost puppy and find it difficult to decide what to do next. About 60% of quitters suffer from this to some extent but the good news is that you really can do something about it.

Keep busy

Arrange to keep yourself busy doing some reasonably pleasant activities for the first week or so. Being absorbed in a creative or satisfying task of some kind will make the time pass more quickly and stop you from wrangling with others. You'll be more self-sufficient and you'll know what you're supposed to be doing from one hour to the next. Uncertainty and indecision can make your irritability worse so good planning will really help. Many people who relapse do so in moments when they are feeling bored, so beware of 'empty time' when you have nothing to occupy you. If you have to wait for an appointment or a friend who is running late then read a book, knit, write letters or think of some other way to pass the time productively. There's no need to paint the entire house or build an extension, just don't sit about waiting for the cravings to come and get you – or they will!

Depression

Most of us get a bit depressed now and again but few people actually suffer from what is known as 'clinical depression' which is a serious condition and one which should be diagnosed and treated by your doctor. When smokers quit, about 60% of them complain about feeling depressed or low during the first month but thankfully it doesn't last long and is not too severe for the majority. Some people have likened the process of giving up smoking, to the process of grieving for a loved one:

> *"At first it was like a bereavement, I'd lost my constant companion for the past 20 years – but after a few weeks I realised that I'd beaten my worst enemy rather than lost my best friend"*

Although it may be an unlikely analogy it does seem that many bereaved people and ex-smokers often claim to have passed through similar stages. The process by which both

groups pass from 'Denial' to 'Acceptance' may well involve a
period of 'Depression', it being a natural and necessary part of
the psychological healing process your mind goes through
when you give up something that's been a part of your daily
routine for so long. It's not much fun when you're in the
middle of it but remember that it *is* temporary and that in a
way it is a stepping stone to freedom.

Beat the blues with rewards

Whilst a certain amount of depression may be unavoidable,
there's certainly no need to wallow in misery! Taking prompt
action and lining up treats and pleasant activities will help to
jog you out of a depressive mood before it gets too bad. Imagine that you've been given a sick child to cosset and care for.
If this were the case you'd spend time planning treats, out-
ings, presents and tempting meals to keep his/her spirits up.
Many of us are good at thinking of ways to please other people
and less adept at looking after ourselves. Now is the time to
put yourself first. If your mood dips then you'll be vulnerable
and more likely to relapse so swing into action and pamper
yourself. Don't wait for other people to recognise your feelings and cheer you up, do it yourself! (For more on rewards
see Chapter 7.)

Challenge the logic of depression

When quitters get into a depressed state of mind they sometimes imagine that without cigarettes there is nothing to look
forward to any more. The future may look grey and bleak so
it's important to recognise these depressive thoughts and
challenge them. Once your addiction to tobacco has been
broken you will return to being your old self and you will
have fun again. Day to day living will be full of the usual highs
and lows and if you regard your new smoke-free status as an
opportunity rather than a threat, you may find life even more
rewarding than before.

Light-headedness

Some of the quitters I've met have complained that in the first day or two after stopping smoking they feel 'spaced out', almost as if they've been drugged. They find it difficult to concentrate at work as a result and often worry that they'll make mistakes while driving or carrying out some other important task. Research has shown that this is a problem for about 10% but the good news is that it's short-lived. After about 48 hours this light-headed feeling goes away, which suggests that it may have something to do with the drop in carbon monoxide levels and an increased oxygen supply to the brain. Either way it's a good sign and nothing to worry about, even if it is a bit inconvenient and disconcerting. One member of a group I was counselling (who came to be called 'The Rubber Man' because of his laid-back approach) actually enjoyed this strange 'druggy' feeling and was very disappointed when it wore off!

Poor concentration

Your concentration may be affected for a couple of weeks after stopping but it should return to normal after that. This happens to about 60% of those who quit so don't worry, you're not alone! It stands to reason that while you're putting time, effort and mental energy into giving up smoking, you may not be able to give as much of yourself to other tasks or activities.

Suck it and see ...

If you do find it difficult to concentrate then try not to worry. So what if your work performance isn't 100% or even 50% for a couple of weeks. Giving up smoking is more important to your future health and happiness than a few niggles at work. If you're worried about managing concentration tasks like driving or working at a keyboard then try chewing gum or sucking lollipops (sugar-free if weight is an issue). Somehow the action of sucking seems to help some people to focus better and it'll help to keep your hands and mouth occupied as well.

Disturbed sleep patterns

About a quarter of you may find that you wake up at night for a while after stopping (usually about a week or so). This can be annoying and may make you feel drowsy in the daytime as well but it's nothing to worry about. All of your bodily rhythms have to adapt to your new smoke-free status and, as a result, they may be 'out of whack' for a while. Heavy smokers sometimes wake during the night craving nicotine so continuing to smoke is no guarantee of quiet nights; whatever your normal sleep pattern is, it'll settle down again soon.

Nicotine dreams

If you decide to wear 24-hr nicotine patches (See Chapter 5: Which Treatment?) then your sleep may be a little disturbed as a result of having nicotine in your system all the time. Some people report having vivid 'nicotine dreams' and sleep more fitfully than before but this doesn't happen to everyone. If getting to sleep is a real problem then try gentle remedies like a warm drink and a bath prior to bed before turning to sedatives or sleeping pills which might be hard to come off later. There are some non-addictive sleep preparations available these days so ask your pharmacist or your doctor for advice if you need more help.

'DAMIT'!

Later on in the process of stopping, maybe after a few weeks, you may have dreams in which you relapse and have a cigarette. This happened to me and many others have described the same thing. They wake in the morning in a panic, thinking that they've 'blown it' and are greatly relieved to find that it was only a dream. Dr Peter Hajek of the Royal London Hospital has called this phenomenon 'DAMIT', meaning 'Dreams of absent-minded transgressions'. The fact that quite a lot of people have these dreams some time after stopping would seem to suggest that they are part of their subconscious adjustment to non-smoking. It may be that at some deeper level your mind is recognising that an important change has taken place and that now smoking is no longer what you really want. Whatever the underlying cause, there's no need to worry if you do get dreams like these as they will pass quite soon.

Anxiety

Recent research suggests that anxiety may not be a true withdrawal symptom but rather a response to the process of stopping itself. Just before the Quit Day people get extremely anxious but those who manage to stay smoke-free for 4 weeks or more report that their anxiety levels fall dramatically compared with before they stopped. This may have a lot to do with the fact that smokers are more stressed than non-smokers. Once they've got through the first 3 or 4 weeks, they realise that it is possible to exist from day to day without tobacco and that they may in fact succeed, which lessens their anxiety about the whole thing. By contrast, those who try to control their addiction by cutting down complain of an increase in anxiety levels. It's difficult to maintain 'low-level smoking' if you're addicted, as it means being in withdrawal for quite a lot of time each day. This may well be why most people can't sustain this kind of rationing system and end up going back to smoking just as much (if not more) than before.

Craving (urges to smoke)

Craving for a smoke tends to be the most troublesome aspect of quitting and, like other symptoms, it's usually at its worst during the first week and then it gradually becomes less strong and less frequent as the weeks go by. Early on you may feel as though you are craving almost continuously but a bit later (probably after the first week), you'll find that you can identify specific craving episodes or 'attacks'. These usually last for about 3 minutes and have been likened to labour pains in that they build up in intensity, rising to a kind of 'crescendo of desire' before slackening off and going away again. Cravings can be triggered by certain situations (e.g. drinking in a bar) but once you've successfully coped with that situation a few times it will gradually lose its power to make you crave. As the weeks pass these attacks will get further and further apart and you'll get more 'time-off' in between them when you are able to get on with other things without thinking about cigarettes. This is a foretaste of the kind of freedom from tobacco that will soon be yours.

Urge surfing

In the US an addictions researcher called Alan Marlatt once came up with a novel idea for 'riding out' craving attacks which has been useful to some of the people I have counselled in the past. He suggests that when you feel an urge to smoke coming upon you, you should visualise it as a rising wave and imagine yourself surfing on the back of it. The basic idea is that you meet the challenge of the craving and go with it, keeping in mind that it will be over in a few minutes and you will have beaten it for the time being. This might help or, if that's too whacky for you, you can try all manner of distraction techniques to get you through that crucial three minutes. Go outside, take twenty deep breaths, stand on your head or whistle Dixie if you like, just so long as you don't smoke! Check out the list of Relapse Prevention Tips towards the end of the book and try out a few. They may not make everything magically easy, but if they help you to beat a craving attack then you'll live to fight another day and you'll be one step closer to your goal of stopping for good.

'When will the cravings stop?'

This is a question that I've been asked at least a hundred times by anxious quitters who are about to take the plunge. The answer is that for most people cravings are much less of a problem by about the 3- to 4-week point and they gradually die away over the weeks and months that follow. It's not possible to give an individual a specific date when all cravings will have ceased but nearly all of the successful stoppers I've worked with have found that after about 3 months cravings are very occasional. When you encounter situations in which you would have smoked you may still get a kind of 'flashback craving' some time after stopping but it's usually short-lived and once you've registered mentally that that's what's happening, it'll probably go away quite quickly. Eventually cravings become more like memories of wanting to smoke and are brief, fleeting thoughts that are relatively easy to dismiss from your mind. Some (rather unhelpful) people are fond of saying things like, 'My friend gave up smoking 10 years ago and she says that she still craves every day' which can be very discouraging to a quitter in the early stages. My response to such a statement would be to point out that the friend in question is either:

(a) superhuman for having withstood intensive daily
       cravings for so long

OR

(b) not experiencing craving in the same way as a person
       who has only just stopped smoking

In any case, this person has clearly managed to stay smoke-free so it can't be as bad as all that ... If you worry a lot about cravings getting the better of you, or you've had problems with them before, then all the more reason to think seriously about using NRT which will reduce them significantly if properly used. It won' t make them go away altogether, but if you visu-alise your cravings as a mountain peak, then NRT will chop the top off it for you and make your first weeks without tobacco much more manageable.

Constipation

Some stoppers report that they suffer from some degree of constipation although I don't have exact figures to quote on this one. If it happens to you don't worry as it will sort itself out in time. Try eating fibre-rich foods to help your digestive system along and wait for things to settle back into a normal pattern. If the problem is severe visit your doctor who may prescribe a laxative preparation to be used in the short-term.

Coughing and 'chestiness'

Many people who stop smoking experience some bronchial problems in the weeks and months after their Quit Day. For those who stop mainly in order to avoid health problems, this can be tiresome and worrying. It might seem a trifle ironic that you're likely to suffer from *more* coughs and colds *after* stopping smoking, but it's actually a sign that your body is working to clear out the tar and matter that has been left behind by your cigarettes over the years. Tiny hairs, called 'cilia', line the respiratory tract, and in non-smokers they work in a wave-like motion to 'flick' impurities up and out of the person's body. This cleaning system prevents potentially dangerous substances from reaching the lungs, but in regular smokers the cilia will have been 'killed off' by the constant intake of smoke and poisonous chemicals. The good news is that once you stop smoking the body's recovery processes swing into action. The cilia grow back and start working to dislodge all the tar etc. that has built up in your chest over the years. Chest infections may occur during this 'cleaning out' phase, when things are moving about a bit internally and much will obviously depend on the condition of your lungs before you stopped, but try not to worry about coughing and congestion. It will probably ease as time goes by and it's a good sign that your body is working to reverse the damage it has suffered.

Hunger and weight-gain

If you're one of the millions of smokers who'd like to stop but hang back because of worries about weight-gain then this section is for you! I'd like to be able to comfort you by saying that weight-gain is not a likely problem after quitting but both you and I know that for a great many people it is. About 70% of stoppers find that their appetite increases for 10 weeks or more after they pack up smoking and their weight typically goes up as well.

A common misconception about eating and smoking is that people eat as a substitute for having something (i.e. a cigarette) in their mouths but the truth is that nicotine actually causes people to lose weight. It speeds up the basic metabolic rate and so you burn up more calories as a smoker, and when you stop smoking, your metabolism slows down so that fewer calories are used up. Nicotine also acts as a mild appetite-supressant, reducing your appetite – but don't make the mistake of thinking that smoking is a universal cure for obesity. As you get older, smoking will adversely affect your ability to exercise and you're likely to become less and less mobile. As a result you'll expend less energy and so your weight may rise even though you continue to smoke. At worst you could end up fat, sick and a smoker!

When you stop smoking your sense of taste and smell improve a great deal and so most quitters find that they enjoy their food more. This enhanced enjoyment can lead to increased consumption which can lead to weight-gain.

'How much weight will I put on?'

The average weight-gain following smoking cessation is between 3 and 10 lbs but much depends on you. There's no need to put on huge amounts of weight but if you get depressed about having put on a bit and then go on a mammoth 'eating jag' you could get locked into cycle of comfort eating and weight-gain. Your attitude to a relatively small gain can therefore govern what happens next.

How to minimise weight-gain after stopping

It is possible to control the amount of weight gained after stopping smoking but it's important to get your priorities straight first:

1. In the vast majority of cases, the health benefits of giving up smoking far outweigh (if you'll pardon the expression!) the negative effects of any weight increases.
2. If you expect yourself to give up smoking and go on a strict diet at the same time then you are more likely to relapse as you'll feel deprived on all fronts. Don't try to be superhuman, take one thing at a time.
3. When you are safely clear of your tobacco addiction you can turn your attention to shifting any excess weight and, with the behaviour-change skills you've mastered, you'll be better able to slim down again later.

Sensible snacking

Given that you may well start nibbling (or indeed guzzling!) at and between meals in the first few weeks after stopping, it's as well to try and make some healthier snack choices from the outset. Biscuits and cookies are nice but they don't last long in your mouth and they do tend to hang around on your hips! Try the following snacks if you're determined not to put on too much weight but know you'll need to nibble:

Sugar-free lollipops (these last ages and are low-cal so don't worry if people call you Kojak!)

Dried Fruit

Crispbread (with a low-fat spread of some kind)

Rice-cakes (you can also get low-cal chocolate-coated rice-cakes at health food shops)

Chewing gum (nicotine or regular)

Fresh fruit (dipped in melted chocolate and chilled in the fridge if you have a sweet tooth or as it comes. Try exotic

varieties you wouldn't normally buy such as kiwi or
mango)

Iced lollies (some are very low in calories and they last a
while in the mouth)

Mints (go for low-sugar varieties whenever possible)

Glucose tablets (these are only about 10 cals per tablet and
they may also help with craving as discussed earlier)

Raw vegetables (e.g. carrots) if you can be bothered to chop
them up put some in a 'nibble box' and carry it about with
you

Food as a reward

If you enjoy food (and most of us do) then you can use special
meals and food treats as a way to spur yourself on. Lovingly
prepared meals that contain a range of delicious flavours can
be eaten and enjoyed at key points, such as the end of your
first 3 days or the first week after your Quit Day. Don't deny
yourself all the good things there are to eat but ration them
carefully and you'll get to enjoy eating without gaining too
much weight. The occasional 'blow-out' will help you celebrate milestones and needn't mean the end of your sensible
eating plans so go on and enjoy your success!

CHAPTER 7

Donkeys, Carrots & the Importance of Rewards

Although many of us flatter ourselves that we are complex creatures with a wide range of intricate motives for the things we do and the paths we choose through life, we are basically like donkeys following carrots. Generally, we need something to look forward to. We'll follow a particular course of action if we can see that it will result in a pleasant (or at least tolerable) outcome, and if we can't see anything nice on the horizon then we slow down, stop or maybe even turn around and go back the other way!

YOU *DO* DESERVE IT!

If you've plucked up the courage to break away from tobacco for good then you deserve to treat yourself. Quitting smoking is the single most important thing you can do for your health and well-being so don't sell yourself short; keep your spirits up with a few treats and you'll be more likely to stay off for good. Small, frequent rewards are great for the first few days but why not set your sights on something bigger when you've been smoke-free for 3 weeks, 3 months or a year? It's time to put yourself at the top of the list for once, so go on, spoil yourself! Here are two lists of reward suggestions – big and small – but they are just the things that appeal to me and everyone is different so think creatively and add a few of your own ...

12 Small Rewards For the First Few Days/Weeks

1. **Have a nice long heart to heart** on the phone with someone you don't see very often, it feels great to be in touch

2. **Enjoy your new-found sense of smell** and get relaxed at the same time – treat yourself to an aromatherapy massage or bath

3. **If you're a bit of a bookworm**, why not raid the local library or bookshop and stock up on escapist novels or meaty biographies?

4. **Revamp your image** with a new hairstyle and have a manicure while you're at it

5. **Movie buff?** Get a few of your favourite old films out on loan and spend an afternoon on the sofa (tear-jerkers are great for releasing pent-up tension/emotion ...)

6. **Spend a lazy day** in bed with your favourite person!

7. **Buy yourself a beautiful bunch of flowers** and a box of the best chocolates – you're worth it

8. **Make yourself a big bowl of delicious fresh fruit salad** with strawberries, mangos and any other fruits you like. Dip into it whenever you feel like a treat

9. **At the end of a long day's quitting**, why not get hold of your favourite comedy video and watch it with a friend – there's nothing like a good giggle to help you unwind!

10. **Go and give your kids a big hug** – enjoy the knowledge that you don't have to worry about smelling like an old ashtray anymore and that you're setting them a great example

11. **Take a day off work** and spend it pampering yourself rotten at home, you could finish up by taking a long hot soak in the bath, eating strawberries and sipping cold champagne!

12. **Join a gym or a health club**, you might find that you can do a whole lot more now you're not huffing and puffing all day and soon you'll look like a million dollars!

12 Bigger Rewards For the First Few Weeks/Months

1. **Splash-out** on a new wardrobe and step out in style!

2. **Freshen up the decor** in your house with a new colour scheme, your home will smell clean and you'll be amazed at the difference a couple of pots of paint can make

3. **Take a trip to Paris** or any destination you like for a romantic weekend with your partner!

4. **Realise a childhood fantasy**, drive a racing car or a steam locomotive for a day!

5. **Arrange to get away from it all** with a luxurious mini-break at a health spa

6. **Tickle those taste-buds** with a fantastic blow-out at a local restaurant. Try foods you've never tasted before and broaden your culinary horizons

7. **Book a makeover** and have a set of glamorous photos taken to celebrate the new you!

8. **Throw caution to the wind** and put a down payment on that dream motor-bike/car you've always wanted (Expensive? Yes, but think of all the money you'll save

on cigarettes in the years to come and hey! life is for living isn't it?)

9. **Book up for a night at the theatre/opera** or go and see your favourite band. Follow it up by having dinner at a fancy restaurant with your best friend!

10. **Get down to the travel agents and plan a dream holiday** in Australia or the Seychelles for when you've been smoke-free for a year ...

11. **Clean or buy new curtains and carpets** (get the old smoke and stains out of your home at last!)

12. **Invest some of the money you're saving** on cigarettes in a savings plan that matures in 5 years then enjoy planning what to do with that lump sum when it comes

CHAPTER 8

The STOP! Plan

Your Step-by-step, Daily Guide to Stopping Smoking Successfully

Good preparation and planning will help you to stop smoking and should help you to feel more confident but even the best prepared 'stopper' can get an attack of the 'wobbles' as the Quit Day approaches and the prospect of abstinence looms large on the horizon. This plan will take you through days leading up to stopping, the all-important first day, the first week and then weeks 2 and 3. You can follow it like a diet plan and stick to the advice given to the letter or you can adapt certain elements to suit your lifestyle, that's up to you, but when craving strikes or your mind starts playing tricks on you it'll keep you on track. It's like a road map to help you negotiate your way past obstacles and move through withdrawal to the point when your cravings will have become infrequent and you are savouring the great taste of freedom from the tobacco trap.

COUNTDOWN STARTS:

1 Week before Quit Day

You may have set your quit date ages ago or you might decide today that you'll go for it in 7 day's time, either way you need to begin preparing now. DON'T try and reduce your cigarette consumption at this point, just relax and smoke as you would normally, no more, no less. Your instructions at this stage are to smoke whenever you feel like it. Cutting down or imposing strict rules about where and when you can smoke will probably make you feel edgy and anxious about doing without cigarettes later so take the pressure off and carry on as normal. Start writing a list of the potential benefits of stopping on the following page and add to it over the next few days as you think of things. Some advantages are obvious such as 'more money', 'no smokers' cough' etc., but there are loads more when you think about it. In the second column on the page write down the possible benefits of continuing to smoke and add to that as things occur to you as well. This might sound like a strange thing for me to ask you to do, but there are some candidates for this side of the list and it's best to put them down, e.g. 'not having to stop now'! Identifying and analysing these two lists will help you to explore your feelings about smoking and will remind you that you *do* have a choice about stopping. No one can make you stop if you really don't want to, but if you do then it's as well to get all the angles covered and make a balanced decision. Have a look at the list each day before you go to bed and add any new entries you've thought of that day.

5 Days and counting

If you want to tell people that you're going to stop smoking then now might be a good time to do it. Some people like to keep it to themselves in case things go wrong but others prefer to commit themselves publicly before the event. I don't think it's helpful to insist that you tell everyone you know, but I do recommend telling your nearest and dearest or people that you actually live with. This is because you're going to need as much support as possible on the home front and it'll underline your commitment to going through with it. This may be

The Pros and Cons of Stopping

BENEFITS OF STOPPING SMOKING	BENEFITS OF CONTINUING TO SMOKE

problematic if your partner or a member of the household smokes but it needn't cause confrontation if you approach them diplomatically. Explain that you're really serious about stopping and that while you don't want to cramp their style or make them quit, you do need a bit of cooperation, especially in the first few days. Some loved ones will of course be glad to help but if you can just persuade others not to smoke in front of you or leave cigarettes lying about in the first few days then it'll cut down on temptation and aggravation later on.

4 Days and counting

Time to get in some supplies. Once you've decided on the form of NRT you're going to use (if you're going to use it) then get down to the chemist and get at least a week's supply. It might seem like a lot to pay all in one go but you're investing in your future and you won't be buying cigarettes after the Quit Day so you'll save in the long run. You don't need any additional hassles or uncertainties in the first week so get enough to see you through it comfortably. It doesn't pay to be penny-pinching with NRT as it simply won't work if you don't use enough. Once you've bought your chosen treatment you'll feel better prepared and less scared of withdrawal. If you're planning to do some creative work like drawing or painting to distract you then pop out for the materials now. Books and magazines are excellent for occupying your mind and distracting you in the first few days so it might be an idea to cruise around a bookshop or two as well.

3 Days and counting

At about this time you might start having reservations about stopping. You might get to thinking that now isn't the right time or that a few weeks from now would be a better time to quit. You might feel keen to stop one minute and very luke-warm about it the next. Alternatively you may feel impatient to get started and irritated by having to hold off for a while longer. These feelings are quite normal and are experienced by a great many people in the days just prior to stopping. IGNORE THEM and continue with your planning and preparations. Now would be a very good time to decide what BIG reward you're going to give yourself when you've been smoke-free for 6 months. It could be a holiday in the sun, a new car or a new kitchen, that's up to you but you need to find something that will work as a good incentive and commit yourself to getting it. Put a down payment on it and stick a picture on the fridge to remind yourself of what success will bring. Everybody has some unfulfilled desire lurking at the back of their mind and this is the time to use it!

2 Days and counting

OK, time to step up the preparation a bit. During the first few days post-stopping you're going to need nibbles and distractions so sit down and write a shopping list. 'Nibbles' don't have to be super-fattening as I explained earlier, but the odd little food treat is a good idea for times when you need cheering up. A tempting selection of fruit is a good idea; grapes are handy when you feel that you must pop something into your mouth and now's the time to treat yourself to that selection of exotic fruits you wouldn't normally lash out on. Chocaholics could get some of their favourite variety and put it in the freezer for 'rationing' later. Frozen chocolate can be savoured bit by bit and is less likely to be wolfed down all at once! If you're worried about weight-gain then check out the section on it in Chapter 6 (if you haven't already done so). It's perfectly possible to find low-fat and low-cal nibbles that last longer in the mouth and won't cause you to swell up like a watermelon! Sugar-free lollipops are very helpful as they last for ages and hardly contain any calories at all. Crispbread with low-fat spread is a better option than massive wedges of bread and butter or an endless succession of biscuits! Whatever you choose for the first few days post-quitting, make sure that it's quick and easy to prepare and get your supplies in now. Don't wait until Day 1 as your thinking may not be quite as focused then as it is now! You should already have your supplies of NRT if you're using it; if you haven't, get it today in case of public holidays, early-closing, earthquakes or any other acts of god that might mean you haven't got it in time for Day 1!

Suggested pre-quit shopping list

NRT
Glucose tablets
Nibble foods (refer to the list in the last chapter for more
    ideas)
Chocolate (for treats if you like it)
Fruit juices
Decaffeinated tea & coffee
Herbal teas
Books and magazines to read
Selection of videos guaranteed to make you laugh
Creative hobby materials (e.g. drawing pencils and paper,
    knitting wool & needles)
Mouthwash (to freshen your breath)
Luxury foods (whatever tickles your taste-buds!)
Fresh flowers (to brighten up the house and cheer you up)

The day before your Quit Day

OK, you're nearly there and by now you may be feeling impatient to get on with the job of stopping. You might also be having cold feet and it's as well to watch out for those negative 'turn back now' type thoughts we mentioned earlier. You may find yourself smoking more today as it comes home to you that this *really* is your last smoking day. Many stoppers smoke very intensively, as though they can somehow stockpile vast amounts of nicotine in their systems to last the next ten years!

It doesn't really matter if you find yourself doing this, the important thing to do is relax because you *are* well prepared and you *can* get it right this time. You know from your smoking diary and your list of proven tactics for trigger situations that there are many ways to beat the cravings and if you're using NRT as well then you're armed to the hilt! All that remains now is to enjoy today as much as possible and focus on your reasons for stopping. You'll soon be free of tobacco addiction, which is wonderful.

Activity planning

Your last preparation task is to write down all your planned activities for Days 1, 2 and 3. Make a list of tasks or leisure activities and the time periods in which you plan to do them. It may not be possible to be exact about all your activities. Unexpected situations may arise at some point during that 3-day period but it's vital that you know what you're going to be doing from one hour to the next and that you don't end up twiddling your thumbs and inviting craving to strike. It's also vital to build in rest/reward breaks so that you won't work yourself to death or end up feeling tired and miserable. I've prepared this example of an Activity Plan to give you the general idea but you can adapt it to suit your lifestyle. The contents of the plan will of course depend on your work routine and the activities you enjoy when not at work so you'll have to work out how to incorporate reward breaks at regular intervals during the day. You'll need to make a plan for each of the first few days, after which point you should be able to get by without writing it all down.

Before bed

Your final piece of preparation must be done before you go to sleep tonight and that is to throw away all your cigarettes, pipes, rolling tobacco, papers, cannabis (see the special section for dope-smokers if this is a problem), lighters and smok-

Activity Plan Day 1 (example)

TIME	ACTIVITY
7.00 am	Breakfast
8.00 am	Kids to school
9.00 am	Shopping
10.00 am	Reward break
11.00 am	Housework
12.00 pm	Writing/reading
1.00 pm	Lunch and reward break
2.00 pm	Housework
3.00 pm	Writing/reading
4.00 pm	Reward break
5.00 pm	Collect kids
6.00 pm	Cook kids' meal
7.00 pm	Relaxing bath/shower
8.00 pm	Evening meal plus treat
9.00 pm	Watch funny video
10.00 pm	Plan next day's activities and go to bed

ing paraphernalia. Some people also throw out their ashtrays which isn't a bad idea but if you don't want to do that then put them in a cupboard out of sight. You won't need these things at all as a non-smoker and having them around is just asking for trouble! I've known quite a few stoppers who've kept 'token' cigarettes about the place on the basis that if they have tobacco in the house it's somehow clearer that they are 'choosing' not to smoke. Unfortunately many of these same smokers will relapse, because when they were vulnerable the means to smoke was only yards away. Relapse comes about when VULNERABILITY meets OPPORTUNITY and if the temptation to smoke is strong then the presence of 'smokeables' makes it even worse. Be kind to yourself and avoid unnecessary temptation by ditching everything now. Try and have a good night's sleep and congratulate yourself on getting this far. Many people 'chicken out' (I mean this kindly you understand) before they get to the Quit Day, so you've already overcome some important psychological hurdles and if you've done the preparation work suggested you're in an excellent position to make a go of it.

NB: If you're throwing away unused cigarettes then soak them with water first or you may find yourself rummaging through

'I accidentally stumbled across a cigarette my wife had carelessly left lying around'

the bin tomorrow and scraping baked beans off them! (I speak as one who has done this on a number of sad occasions and it's a pretty degrading situation to find yourself in.) Remember also to check through old coats and bags and your car for any forgotten supplies. Once you've stopped smoking these 'lost' cigarettes may start 'singing to you' or pop up when you open a drawer or reach into your bag so find them now and save yourself trouble later.

And finally ... If you've opted for 24-hour nicotine patches then now's the time to slap one on so that it will have kicked in nicely by the time you wake up. If not then put your NRT supplies (be they patches, gum or whatever) together with this book ready for the morning. That way, when you wake up you'll feel more confident.

How to Survive Day 1 (without smoking or going crazy!)

Most people who relapse do so on Day 1 or in the first 3 days after stopping. I'm not saying this to depress you, but rather to emphasise the importance of getting through this phase without smoking at all (no, not even a puff!). After the 3/4-day barrier things get markedly easier for most people but for now your task is to take it slowly and carefully. Follow your Activity Plan and refer to your list of tips and strategies for your top ten dangerous situations. All your careful preparations will come into their own and you should feel that you've got some 'ammo' for the battle by now.

WHEN YOU WAKE UP

NRT users should open up their supplies as soon as they get up. Don't hang about thinking you'll try some gum or put on a patch later, have some now! That way it will start working sooner and help you on your way.

BREAKFAST

Whatever your views on the merits of breakfast as a meal, you need to have some today. Making it will distract you and give you something to occupy your hands and mind. Eating it will mean that your blood sugar stays higher throughout the morning, which will keep you on a more even keel both mentally and physically. Slow-release carbohydrates like toast or cereals will sustain you for longer but why not go mad and have an egg or some fruit as well? Now is not the time to deny yourself, so have something you like and eat a reasonable amount, even if your brain isn't quite working properly and it tastes like cardboard! After a few days your body will start expecting something at breakfast time and you'll probably come to enjoy it more than you thought possible. If not you can always abandon eating it when you've safely negotiated the withdrawal phase.

WHAT TO DRINK

Tea and coffee might make you want to smoke more than other drinks so have some fruit juice, milk or herbal tea with your breakfast just for now or switch to a decaffeinated version of your favourite beverage. If you really can't face starting the day without your regular caffeine hit then limit it to one cup for now and eat something with it. Once breakfast is finished don't sit there clock-watching or wondering what's missing, you know what's missing! Get up, clear up the dishes and prepare for the day ahead. Busy mums and dads will probably be occupied with the school run etc., but if your time is your own in the mornings then consult your Activity Plan and get on with the first section right away.

Day 1 Activity & Reward Schedule

WAKE-UP

Start using NRT (if you've chosen to use it to help you stop) and make breakfast. Eat breakfast, clear away and dress.

2 HOURS OF ACTIVITY

(e.g. kids' run followed by work or house-cleaning, shopping, gardening etc.)

★ **Craving Tip**: Don't revisit your decision to stop smoking. It was a good one and there's no point wrangling with yourself over it now. Accept that the next few days will be a bit unusual and that you might feel odd but remember that you won't die as a result of stopping smoking!

REWARD BREAK 1 (10 TO 15 MINS)

A small break here is very important. Have a drink and something to nibble. Change your activity and do something for your self for a short while: read a book or a magazine, take a stroll or sit down and listen to the radio if you've been on your feet. Try to get away by yourself (preferably away from smokers!) If necessary go off to the rest-room or leave the building if it's hard to engineer a smoke-free break at work. If you feel stressed out try the 'fantasy cigarette' breathing exercise and congratulate yourself on having got to this point. You're doing really well!

★ **Craving Tip**: Suck a sugar-free lollipop, have a piece of gum (nicotine or otherwise) or have a piece of fruit with a drink of juice when you feel a craving coming on.

2 HOURS OF ACTIVITY

(e.g. work, gardening, cooking etc.) If possible do something different from before your reward break and focus on getting through until lunch-time. Keep nibbles or gum with you and use as required. If you're using nicotine gum, spray, Minitab or Inhalator then keep dosing yourself at regular intervals. Don't try to get by on too little or you won't be giving the product a chance to help you. If people offer you a cigarette, decline politely, saying something like 'not just at the moment thanks'. That way they won't be so keen to engage you in a long conversation about the perils of stopping!

★ **Craving Tip**: Remember that craving attacks usually last for just a couple of minutes, they reach a peak of intensity and then slacken off, a bit like a cresting wave. Practice 'riding out' this wave like a surfer and learn to recognise the signs of a craving attack early.

LUNCH-BREAK

(1 hour if possible or whatever you can manage but not less than 30 mins)

Get a change of scene to freshen you up. Go outside and take some nice deep breaths to calm you down and get some lunch. If you're preparing it yourself then take a bit of time to get something tasty together. Now is the time to get out some of the nice food you bought over the last couple of days. If you're eating out then go to a restaurant you haven't been to before or somewhere a bit nicer than usual. Choose something good and take the time to eat and enjoy it while reading or chatting with a sympathetic non-smoker (if there's one handy). You've done brilliantly to get to this point so you deserve a luxury nibble or a small extravagance once lunch is over.

★ **Craving Tip**: Most stoppers crave a cigarette after eating so don't dawdle at the table once you've eaten. Get up and get active again. Brush your teeth if possible and get busy with something immediately.

2 HOURS OF ACTIVITY

NB: Remember to keep using your NRT and don't worry if you feel a bit light-headed at some point today. Your brain is getting more oxygen than it has been used to and that can be a 'heady' sensation! It's a good sign and your powers of concentration will return to normal within a day or two. Some people actually enjoy this sleepy, slightly 'drugged' feeling so if it happens to you try and 'go with the flow' and relax as much as possible.

★ **Craving Tip**: You may notice treacherous negative thoughts creeping into your mind at odd times during the day. The little 'tobacco devil' in your head will use every trick in the book to persuade you to crack up so watch out for these 'relapse ideas' and squash them by talking to yourself (out loud is good). Counter negative ideas with positive logic and treat yourself to another small reward if necessary.

REWARD BREAK 2

(5 to 15 mins) Only a little while to go until the evening so keep yourself busy but be aware that you'll be getting tired. Don't overdo it! Stopping smoking is hard work and you're bound to feel it towards the end of the day. Use some more NRT to keep the cravings at bay (if you're on any form other than patches) and start looking forward to a good dinner and a pleasant evening of self-indulgence. Have a drink (some juice or a hot drink if you prefer) and a sweet nibble of some sort.

★ **Craving Tip**: If you feel down phone someone supportive
for a morale boosting chat. If being on the phone makes
you crave then hold the receiver in one hand and a pen in
the other. Doodle while you talk (try not to draw
cigarettes if possible!) and have a glass of water nearby to
sip. Explaining to someone how you feel will release
tension and help you to move on.

TEA/DINNER TIME

The transition from day to evening can be a real stumbling
block so be prepared. Many smokers associate getting home
and putting their feet up with reaching for the cigarette
packet. If you have children and/or a meal to prepare then
you'll be quite busy which may keep you out of trouble but
don't wait too long to have a rest-break. Put your feet up, use
some more NRT if necessary and read or watch TV for a few
minutes. If that's too difficult then go out for a short walk in
the fresh air to revive your spirits. You've nearly done a whole
day and if you can do one then you can do another etc. etc.
Look after yourself and plan a relaxing evening. Have a long
luxurious soak in the bath, eat a delicious meal in front of a
funny video and keep using NRT to help you through. A relatively early night with a good book will help you to de-stress
and prepare for Day 2. You've done absolutely brilliantly today
so give yourself some credit!

DAYS 2 & 3

Keep to a planned routine
You will need to follow the same pattern of meals, activity sessions and reward breaks as you did for Day 1 but you should
ring the changes a bit when it comes to rewards. Plan to have
larger rewards at the end of the day when you may feel at a

low ebb· and keep taking your NRT at regular intervals or applying your patches when the pack says you should. If friends or work-mates are making life difficult then refer to the section on 'Sabotage' for advice on what to do. Other people can be a help or a hindrance but if you stay true to yourself they can't knock you off course.

Beware of Day 2 blues

Some stoppers find that they begin to feel rather low at the end of Day 2 when negative thoughts creep in just as nicotine levels fall. You may start to think that nothing will ever be the same again and that it's all getting a bit too much like hard work now that the novelty has slightly worn off. If this happens to you on Day 2 or Day 3 then keep those rewards coming and remind yourself that after 4 days you'll get more 'time off' from the cravings and that things will become more manageable. It's very rewarding to discover, at the end of the first week, that you've been busy doing something and haven't actually thought about smoking (or not smoking) for a whole hour or more. It's a taste of the freedom that will soon be yours and with every craving that you manage to beat off, your confidence and skill will grow.

Tears before bedtime?

Stopping smoking may make you cry! Don't worry if this happens as it's quite common and is all part of the process. Saying goodbye to something that's been with you through thick and thin for years and years is an emotional business and the strain of staying smoke-free may take its toll on your emotions. Crying is actually an excellent way of relieving stress so you'll probably feel much better after a good old-fashioned bawl!

Lashing out?

Irritability and irrational anger are common symptoms in the first few days. If you find that you're getting annoyed by little things or 'blowing your stack' at friends and family, try not to worry. If possible avoid conflict situations by:

(a) leaving the room
(b) leaving the house
(c) agreeing with the person who's got your goat (it'll be hard for them to keep arguing if you stop)

If you have fallen out with others because of your 'short fuse' try to get it all in perspective. For one thing they'll probably forgive you quite readily as they know that it's tough for you at the moment. Most arguments start with something pretty trivial so it's unlikely that the fate of the nation rests on the outcome of your latest 'spat'. Put it behind you and move on, your irritability will subside soon anyway.

Early benefits
By the end of Day 2, your carbon monoxide levels will have fallen to those of a non-smoker, even if you've been puffing away for years. Your heart will be under less strain as a result and your skin colour will start to improve as the blood supply becomes richer in oxygen. If possible get a carbon monoxide test done at your local surgery and see the difference that a couple of days can make.

THE 3-DAY BARRIER

It has often been said that the number 3 is important when you are involved in the task of giving up smoking. I can't remember who first came up with this idea but it does seem to be the case that a great many people experience difficulties at the 3-day mark and that if you can win through to days 4/5 then your chances of long-term success are greatly improved. This may be because of falling nicotine levels which 'bottom-out' at around this point. It might also be that after 3 days of hard work fighting cravings and feeling 'odd' some people lose heart and run into tricky situations when their mood is low. Whatever the cause, the best plan is to buoy yourself up at this point with a really good reward. If you celebrate your achievement in getting this far and remember that from here on in things will get easier then you're less likely to fall by the wayside. Order a sumptuous take-away or splash out on a new outfit. Book that holiday you've been dreaming of or treat yourself to a massage. You are the best judge of what will cheer you up so I won't suggest ideas that appeal to me ad infinitum. It's time for you to get creative and take responsibility for your mood rather than waiting around for the cravings to come and get you. Some ex-smokers have said that stopping is a bit like finally growing up because it involves taking charge of your own destiny in a mature manner rather than forever running away or reaching for your 'security blanket' which in this case is a cigarette.

DAY 7

Hurrah, hooray, whoopee and three cheers for you! Reaching the end of your first week is an important milestone, an awe-inspiring achievement and, at the risk of sounding repetitive, you deserve a reward for getting there! Friends and family may be around to congratulate you, but if not, let me be the first to say, well done! It might be helpful to spend a few minutes looking back over the last few days and considering any highs and lows that stand out in your mind. If it's been mostly lows then you've done brilliantly to get through it and, if there have been times that weren't so bad (or were even quite reasonable), you may have begun to believe that there is light at the end of the tunnel after all. Ask yourself the following questions:

1. Am I craving as much or as often now as I was during the first 3 days?

2. Which symptoms of withdrawal (i.e. irritability, lack of concentration) are still a problem and which have slackened off over the past few days?
3. Which strategies worked best for me when I was tempted to smoke?
4. Am I still using enough NRT to help me ward off unnecessary cravings?
5. Am I looking after myself properly? (i.e. eating regularly, not taking on more work than I can handle and getting plenty of sleep)

I'm a firm believer in adopting the 'if it ain't broke don't fix it' philosophy if you are successfully getting on with your life without smoking. On the other hand, if you are having trouble with a particular withdrawal symptom, such as stress build-up or excessive eating, then now is a good time to re-read the section on dealing with withdrawal and adjusting your strategies or trying new ones. Act now and at least you'll know that you're tackling the problems. That way the psychological addiction is less likely to 'hook you back' with the following excuses for relapsing:

'There's no point in stopping smoking if I'm so ratty my friends can't stand me'

'There's no point in stopping smoking if I'm going to be the size of a house'

'There's no point in stopping smoking if I can't do my job properly'

Remember that all withdrawal symptoms are temporary and that you can take practical steps to reduce their severity.

Back to the bottle?
Alcohol could prove to be your undoing if you allow it so it pays to be careful, but, if you enjoy the odd drink (or 3!) then

there's no need to feel completely deprived. No one is saying that you have to give up everything at once and if you work alcohol into your reward system it could actually help you to stop. Why not plan to have some of your favourite 'tipple' at the end of Day 3 or the first week? Provided you don't go overboard and have it somewhere where there is no tobacco around to tempt you, you can enjoy its 'relaxing' effects and go off to sleep without having blown it. Going to a bar might be too risky at this stage but don't worry, your social life will go back to normal in time and you won't have to become a hermit!

WEEK 2

It's important that when you head into your second week you remember to keep using your NRT and the strategies that have kept you smoke-free so far. You will probably find that you're not craving as often as you did during the first 3 days but for many people the second week can feel like hard going. The novelty of being smoke-free may have worn off to some extent and some stoppers experience a kind of depression at about this stage which we may as well call **Week 2 Blues**. There's no rule that says you will definitely suffer from this of course, but just in case you do it's as well to be prepared for it with extra treats and mood-enhancing strategies such as exercise and talking things through with someone supportive. Don't bottle up negative feelings, get them out and by expressing them with someone else you may find that they ease off or go away altogether. Some ex-smokers have observed that at this stage of the game the future seems like:

*'An endless succession of dreary days with nothing
to look forward to'*

but this 'bereavement' stage of mourning for your lost cigarette 'friend' is probably a necessary part of the process of leaving tobacco behind. The good news is that by Week 3 the clouds tend to lift and things often look considerably brighter. Most withdrawal symptoms start to ease off by about the 3- or 4-week mark as your system acclimatises to its new smoke-free status. After this point not smoking begins to feel more 'normal', mentally as well as physically. Some people actually get quite euphoric about the whole thing at this point as they begin to realise that they really are breaking free.

WEEKS 3/4

OK, you're doing really well and by now the cravings should be more manageable and less frequent on the whole. At this point you need to start looking forward more and accepting that your life will be different from now on. Don't wait to start enjoying new activities, start doing them now! If you've put on weight in the last 3 weeks then you may want to step up the amount of exercise you take and reduce the fat content of your diet a bit but don't do anything too extreme! You're still vulnerable so watch out for dangerous situations and don't deprive yourself of all your treats just yet.

Re-entering society

If you've been avoiding the pub, your favourite bar or certain friends who smoke since your Quit Day then now may be the time to consider returning to them. Only you can judge the possible effect these places or people may have on you, so wait until you feel ready and arm yourself with NRT supplies or nibbles beforehand. Once you've encountered a 'trigger' situation once or twice and managed not to smoke it will gradually lose its power to tempt you. You'll become 'desensitised' to the sight or smell of other people smoking as time goes by and so won't have to avoid social events etc. for too long.

CHAPTER 9

Making it Stick!

When you've successfully managed to do without tobacco for 3 or 4 weeks you're on the threshold of long-term success and have invested a good deal of time and effort in your bid to become a non-smoker. It would be a great shame to have to do it all over again but, as many a smoker will tell you, it's all too easy to fall back into the smoking trap if you allow yourself to believe that it's worth risking a crafty puff. The information in this chapter will help you to avoid relapsing or, if you've cracked up in the past, it may help you to understand why and avoid it next time round.

Most relapses occur early on in the quitting process, many happen in the first week or even on the first day and they are often connected with negative moods like boredom and anger although they may be triggered by celebrations or happy events as well. People who have relapsed after days or weeks of non-smoking often feel really ashamed about it:

'I couldn't believe I'd wasted all that effort after a whole week of not smoking. I relapsed at work when someone offered me a cigarette in the staff canteen. I don't even know why I smoked the first one and then after that I felt so cheesed off with myself and really disappointed. People who had been encouraging me before were quite nice about it but I could see them thinking "she's got no will-power" and that made me feel even more depressed about it.'

IF AT FIRST ...

However annoying it may be to have to start all over again, relapses can give you useful information that can help you succeed next time around. What you need to do is analyse your last relapse, ask yourself where you were at the time, what sort of mood you were in, who you were with and what thoughts were going through your head. The answers should give you clues about your individual weak points and with good planning you could avoid being in the same situation after your next quit. Here's what happened to one stopper I talked to:

Anatomy of a relapse:

Where did it happen?
In the staff canteen at work

Who were you with?
My friend and long-time smoking partner, Marie

How long after stopping did it happen?
2 weeks

How did you feel at the time?
A bit stressed out as it was a busy day in the office

What thought went through your mind just before you relapsed?
I thought, 'I'll only have this one, I deserve something right now'

How did you feel just after?
I had a sort of sinking feeling about what I'd done and the cigarette made me feel a bit 'woozy'.

So, what do these answers tell us about this smoker's relapse? Well, for one thing she was probably still too vulnerable to spend her work breaks with an old smoking pal who was likely to offer her a cigarette! She might have been able to cope with that situation after 3 weeks or so, but at 2 weeks she wasn't ready for it.

The fact that she was feeling "a bit stressed" probably made her more vulnerable and it might have helped if she'd found a different way of relaxing on her break – maybe by going outside, having something comforting to eat or reading a magazine. This would have helped her to calm down without her having to resort to a cigarette.

Celebrate your achievements

After a whole 2 weeks of not smoking this lady certainly did deserve a reward of some kind. It's possible that if she'd already planned a special treat to celebrate this milestone (like a new dress or a meal out with a non-smoking friend) then looking forward to it might have helped her get through to the end of the day.

Build up your motivation again

The important thing for our relapser to remember at this point is that she *did* manage without smoking for 14 days which was excellent, and that next time, with good planning, she may well succeed in becoming a non-smoker. After a relapse it's a good idea to set a new quit date in a few weeks' time and to work on building your motivation up again as it approaches. Bashing yourself over the head about past mistakes doesn't get you very far but a common-sense approach to avoiding relapse can work wonders.

Beware of the 3 C's

CURIOSITY
'I wonder what a cigarette would be like after all this time'

COMPLACENCY
'I'm safe now that I haven't smoked for a few weeks'

CONTROL
'I've learned to control my smoking now, so I can have the odd puff '

Unfortunately, many quitters fall into one or more of these types of thought pattern which lead inevitably to experimentation with the odd cigarette here and there. These odd ones soon become daily events, and before they know it, they're back in the smoking trap. To avoid this happening to you, remind yourself of the following:

1. Cigarettes aren't all that nice when you are no longer addicted to nicotine. They give you a slight headache and can make you feel nauseous. This only changes when you are addicted again and you know exactly what that feels like from all your years of smoking.

2. It is never 'safe' to experiment with tobacco smoking. Nicotine in tobacco is highly addictive and your best bet is to leave it alone entirely. It doesn't matter how long you've been a non-smoker, you are still at high risk of getting re-addicted if you smoke at all.

3. Sadly, you will probably never become a 'social smoker'. Only about 2% of those who ever try tobacco are 'take it or leave it smokers'. The rest of us end up hooked if we dabble so don't take chances thinking that you can control your consumption.

Dope smokers

Those of you who smoke cannabis or marijuana for recreational purposes will know that it's all too easy for dope-smokers to relapse because they sometimes tell themselves that,

'joints don't count'

After smoking cannabis mixed with tobacco in a 'joint', the desire for nicotine resurfaces and the unwary dope-smoker may find himself smoking joint after joint because his desire for tobacco has been 'reawakened'. Joints *do* count, and if you smoke cannabis with tobacco then you run the risk of becoming an addicted smoker again.

Tobacco or cannabis?

Another difficulty for recreational cannabis users is that while they may sincerely wish to give up tobacco because of its effects on their health or their bank balance, they feel less inclined to give up the kind of escapist experience that cannabis offers. If this is a problem for you then my advice would be to avoid using cannabis for the time being. Once you've been tobacco-free for some time (maybe as long as a few months) you can always try it without tobacco (in a pipe perhaps) but you may find that as a non-smoker you find the whole idea less appealing by then. Either way, resolve to avoid it for now and treat situations where others will be smoking joints as highly risky to your smoke-free status in much the same way as you might regard situations involving alcohol. The 'disinhibiting' effects of either substance could undo all your good work so take care.

ALL OR NOTHING

When people try to give up smoking, it's amazing how often an apparently minor lapse (just a quick puff in some cases) can turn into a full-blown relapse and put them right back to square one.

It seems strange that so often someone who has lasted weeks without a single puff of tobacco 'slips up' on one day (maybe by accepting a single cigarette from a friend) and is suddenly back on a pack a day again by the end of the week! Logically speaking, there is no obvious reason why having the odd cigarette should result in returning to regular smoking so quickly but it very often happens that way. So, why does giving up smoking often seem to be such an all-or-nothing thing?

The Abstinence Violation Effect (AVE)

Psychologists who have studied people trying to give up drugs like nicotine have called this tendency to cave in after a lapse the 'abstinence violation effect' (or AVE). This is a fancy way of referring to the psychological process in which someone takes a small amount of the drug in question after going without it for a while and then quickly shifts from thinking:

'I'm doing well, I can beat this thing'

to

'I've blown it, I may as well kipper myself completely!'

A number of recent studies have also provided information that supports this 'all or nothing' syndrome. One study found that among those who had 'detectable smoke' on their breath one week after their Quit Day, only about 7% were not smoking by their third week, whereas almost 50% of those who had not lapsed within the first week, were completely smoke-free two weeks later.

Rat trap

The processes involved in relapses like this may be similar to behaviour observed in laboratory studies of rats (unflattering as that may sound!). In these studies the rats are trained to press a lever in order to receive a small quantity of a drug. The rats will repeatedly press the lever in order to get 'fixes' of an addictive drug (such as heroin, cocaine or nicotine). If when they press the lever the drug doesn't come through then the rat will press more frequently for a short while, and then gradually give up. If, after a period of time without the drug, the rat is given a small amount of that drug again, then it will quickly start pressing the lever again, often at a higher rate than before! Just like a smoker who relapses and then goes back to smoking even more.

Craving

It seems unlikely that these rats are thinking:

'I've blown it now, I may as well go back to 20 cigarettes a day!'

Rather, it may be that a more basic brain mechanism is responsible. It's as if a small quantity of the drug acts as a kind of cue
or 'trigger' and by reminding the rat (or person) of their old
habits it stimulates a strong craving for more.

Beware of the odd puff
The obvious conclusion here is that it is very important to avoid
any kind of slip if you really want to quit smoking for good, no
matter how trivial the occasional cigarette might seem.

Asking for trouble
It sounds like common sense to try to avoid situations that
might make you crave a cigarette or encourage you to smoke.
Strangely though, when people tell me about their relapses
and the events that led up to them, I am often struck by the
'apparently irrelevant' decisions they have often made some
time before smoking that fateful relapse cigarette. People who
are trying to give up smoking sometimes make decisions (possibly quite unconsciously) which are actually designed to
bring them closer to tobacco or put them into situations where
they almost have no choice but to relapse! It's as though the
person is unaware that their plans are so dangerous and they
may be denying the reality of having decided on a particular
course of action because it will make it easier for them to
smoke or provide some sort of justification for relapsing later
on. In other words they are actually planning their own
relapse without realising it!

If you have your cake you'll probably eat it!
The classic example of this kind of 'planned' relapse is the
person who decides to keep their cigarettes with them or close
by when they are trying to stop smoking. When asked why
they are doing this, a common response is, 'it would be harder
to be without them' or, 'just in case of emergencies'. Although
there might be a strand of logic to this decision, I am quite con-

fident that these same people would understand perfectly well that it would not be a good idea to put a chocolate gateau in the fridge at the start of an attempt to lose weight!

No smoke without fire

Another example would be a lady who started lighting her daughter's cigarettes for her in the early stages of her quit attempt, despite the fact that she had never done this before. Whether this was a true attempt at helpfulness (as she claimed) or a subconscious attempt to have a puff, it appears to me that during a quit attempt the mind can play tricks which are (sometimes subconscious) endeavours to sabotage the quit attempt. To help you to guard against these hidden dangers I've prepared this list of 10 common things people do which could well lead to relapse.

10 'apparently irrelevant' things people do when trying to stop smoking (which are really designed to bring them closer to smoking and give them an excuse to crack up!)

1. Keeping a pack of cigarettes in the house
2. Buying duty free cigarettes on holiday
3. Lighting or holding other people's cigarettes
4. Getting so drunk you'll forget you are trying to stop smoking
5. Sitting in the smoking room at work 'just for a chat'
6. Thinking 'it doesn't count if
    (a) it's in a joint
    (b) it's an ultra-light cigarette
    (c) it's someone else's cigarette
    (d) it's on holiday
    (e) no one else sees it'
    (f) you didn't actually buy any cigarettes
7. Offering to 'ook after' someone else's cigarettes

8. Thinking 'there's so much smoke in this bar I might as well smoke myself'

9. When craving for tobacco, popping round to your nearest smoker friend's house for a heart to heart.

10. Picking an argument with your smoker friend/partner knowing that in the end they will tell you to shut up and have a cigarette (and will be in a position to give you one)

SABOTAGE

Social support is very important when you're trying to stop smoking and it can be a real boost when the going gets tough but sometimes friends and family can let you down and they might even cause you to crack up altogether! It's particularly difficult for people whose partners still smoke so if this is the case in your household you really should have a heart to heart with your partner. They don't have to give up with you if they don't feel ready, but if they could at least keep their cigarettes away from you or smoke in another room, it will help.

How to cope when friends and family let you down

You know the situation, you've managed to do without cigarettes for a whole day, a week or maybe even longer. You've been keeping your thoughts positive, you've protected yourself from risky situations and it's beginning to look like this time you might just be getting there, and then it happens – your partner/workmate/so-called best friend actually torpedoes your chances by waving a cigarette in front of your face and saying 'why don't you have one? Surely just one wouldn't hurt'. Alarm bells ring in your head, you can feel a monstrous craving building up and your hard-won confidence drains away in a moment of confusion!

Is it deliberate?

Do they realise how dangerous this is for you? Are they really trying to sabotage your gutsy efforts? You bet your boots they are! The sad fact is that for some smokers your success will feel like a threat and they would rather see you fail than face up to the notion that if you can give up then maybe they ought to have a think about trying too. It's not that they're bad people or anything, maybe they're just not ready to take the plunge but if you really want to make a go of it this time you'd better be prepared for the quit saboteurs!

To help you I've anticipated a couple of typical sabotage comments that you might run into, and prepared these tips on how to negotiate your way past them without cracking up:

The direct offer
This is a pretty standard and bare-faced attempt to get you to break your resolve. You're in the pub or the canteen with a bunch of friends or work-mates. Everyone's having a laugh and out come the cigarettes. The fact that you've been off them for three days hasn't gone unnoticed and it's beginning to make some of your smoking friends feel uncomfortable. So, what do they do? They offer you one of course, they actually get out a packet with one cigarette sticking out temptingly and hold it towards you saying, 'Go on, you know you want to'.

What to do
It might sound obvious but the best solution may be to say 'No thank you, I've given up', unfortunately the determined saboteur may not want to take no for an answer. One quitter became so exasperated by repeated offers of cigarettes even after saying 'no' several times that she eventually took the cigarette, broke it in half and dumped it in the saboteur's drink! 'I know it sounds a bit drastic' she said, 'but they did stop pestering me after that!' Other quitters I've worked with have suggested saying, 'Not just at the moment thanks'. This is a good plan as it suggests that you just don't feel like one at the time and is unlikely to result in some lengthy conversation about the wisdom of quitting or a barrage of

unsolicited advice that may make your cravings even worse than before!

The 'you're so miserable these days, for goodness' sake have a cigarette!' argument

Sadly this form of sabotage often comes from a quitter's nearest and dearest, who many have been supportive to start with, but whose patience has started to wear a little thin. This type of sabotage is more understandable if you really have been behaving like a pit bull terrier with a hangover but there's still no good excuse for it as people ought to be making allowances for your mood if they really care about you.

What to say

If you feel calm enough to assert yourself without getting involved in an all-out war you could try saying,

'I've every right to be bad-tempered when my so-called friends/loved-ones try to make quitting even more difficult for me by urging me to smoke!'

You could also remind them (and yourself) that if you are a bit snappy it's only TEMPORARY, soon you'll be back to your old self and you'll be free of cigarettes at last. Perhaps the best plan is to be honest and up front about your mood. Look your would-be saboteur in the eye and say,

'Yes, you're right, I have been rather snappy lately but smoking isn't the solution. I'm going to get rid of all this stress by:

(a) going for a walk/jog/run in the fresh air
(b) having a good shout/scream/crying session
(c) making myself something nice and indulgent to eat (after all, this is an emergency!)
(d) going to a quiet place on my own to read a book about stopping and get into a positive frame of mind again

or

(e) all of the above!'

Saboteurs may follow your example

Remember, most saboteurs are probably quite jealous that you've managed to make progress while they're still sitting on the sidelines. No one likes to feel left behind and smokers sometimes feel like a dwindling band of social outcasts. In time they may be encouraged by your success and have a go themselves so stick to your guns and don't let the saboteurs succeed!

PREVENTING RELAPSE IN 'HIGH-RISK' SITUATIONS

If you managed to fill out the Smoking Diary section of this book, you may have noticed that there are a number of daily situations in which smoking seems to be 'natural' or in which you feel that the desire to smoke is very strong. To help you cope with these, have a look at the tips and suggestions that follow for some 'classic' high-risk situations/activities. Once you've coped with them once or twice they'll get much easier and you'll start to establish new 'normal' patterns of behaviour within about 3 weeks so things will feel less strange.

The tea or coffee-break situation

Many smokers have a cigarette with a drink of tea/coffee. Consider changing what you drink; fruit juice may remind you of smoking less than tea or coffee does and will help to supplement your vitamin C intake (smokers are often a bit low on vitamin C anyway). You could also change the timing of your drink breaks to help vary the routine and cut the link with smoking. Try swapping the hand you hold your drink in and make sure that you have something to play with whilst you have a cup of tea/coffee, to keep your smoking hand occupied (i.e. doodle with a pen, chew a carrot, some gum or a glucose tablet). Caffeine is a drug of similar composition to nicotine and it may increase the withdrawal effects from smoking and trigger your craving for a cigarette. Consider cutting down on the amount of tea/coffee you drink and find a substitute if possible. If you really love your coffee then build it into your programme of rewards and ration it carefully so that you don't drink too much.

Boredom – dead periods of time or waiting situations

Identify causes of boredom and plan strategies of things to do (i.e. read a book, write a letter, exercise etc). Be aware of the dangers of 'dead periods' whilst waiting for someone. This is where your Activity Plans for the first few days will come in handy. Keep them with you so you know what you're supposed to be doing from one hour to the next.

The after a meal situation

Establish a new after-dinner routine (i.e. wash up immediately, move to another room etc.) and if possible save up a treat for the end of the meal so that you won't sit around feeling deprived. An ice-cream or a sweet treat of some kind would be ideal, or maybe a piece of fruit that you can eat 'on the hoof'. The latter has the added advantage of getting you away from the table. In the evening, plan to watch a good show on TV after your meal or do something creative and absorbing like sewing, drawing, etc.

The driving situation

Some smokers believe that cigarette smoking helps them to relax at the wheel and makes them better drivers! There's no basis for this however – in fact smoking when driving is dangerous! I well remember lighting a cigarette at the wheel and an occasion when, as I went to take it from my mouth, my fingers slipped to the end of it, knocking the burning tip down the front of my shirt! How I managed to control the car as it burned my flesh is anyone's guess but before giving up I was genuinely worried about my ability to drive without smoking. If you fear that you may plough into a bus queue or shoot a few stop signs, try to distract yourself from thinking about smoking by listening to the radio or the cassette player. Singing along with your favourite music will help your breathing and prevent tension build-up. Don't worry if you have a voice like a 'cat's chorus' as no one will know what you sound like as long as you don't have a passenger. If you do then talking to them will help to take your mind off cigarettes anyway. Sucking a sugar-free lollipop can really help in this situation too. It'll leave your hands free and last for ages. Somehow the action of sucking seems to help you concentrate, and when you finish the lollipop you can always chew the stick!

The telephone situation

Keep a notebook and pen near the phone so that you can doodle and change the physical position you normally adopt when phoning, maybe by holding the 'phone in your other hand. Find something to fiddle with whilst you are phoning (a toy, worry beads, an elastic band, bit of Blu-Tack, etc.) and have a glass of cold water available to sip.

The alcohol situation

Alcohol could weaken your resolve to stop and stay stopped. Smoking is frequently associated with drinking alcohol so consider changing your drink or cutting down on the amount of alcohol you drink (especially during the first few weeks). Swap hands if you used to smoke with one hand and hold your drink in that hand instead. Use your common sense about going to bars etc. after stopping. You may be able to cope in Week 3 but it's probably a bad idea to go to a wild party on Day 1!

Habits and routines

In the first few days after stopping it will help if you vary your routine in lots of small ways to cut down on the number of habitual 'triggers' that you'll run into. Something as simple as walking a different way to the shops or to work may help to eliminate some cravings and in the early days you need all the help you can get.

CHAPTER 10

Stress-Busting

As I explained at the beginning of this book, smoking doesn't help with stress. It makes you more stressed and only seems to help you unwind because it relieves your withdrawal symptoms for a little while. People who smoke are used to having certain levels of nicotine in their bodies and so tend to feel agitated and irritable when they haven't smoked for a time. Most smokers experience some withdrawal symptoms if they haven't smoked for as little as an hour. When they light up again and get their 'fix' of nicotine, they feel better. Over the years this creates the firm belief in the minds of many smokers that smoking helps with stress and many will be put off trying to stop for years because they mistakenly believe that life will be impossibly stressful without cigarettes.

In the longer term you'll be much calmer as an ex-smoker but in the short-term you will need to learn new and healthier ways to cope with stress during the days and weeks after stopping. This chapter will arm you with a number of stress-reduction techniques and tips for stressful situations. Try them out and you're sure to find some that help. Stress can spiral out of control if we let it, but by using sensible, practical tips to help you control it you can make even the most stressful situation easier to manage. Once you've mastered these techniques you'll find that you no longer need to reach for a cigarette when an unexpected crisis erupts in your life and you'll be far less likely to relapse further down the line.

MASTER THE ART OF RELAXATION

Relaxation is a skill that takes time to learn – practice the simple deep-breathing exercises that follow at times when you are not stressed and then you'll be an old hand at them if a stressful situation arises later.

Exercise 1: Progressive Muscle Relaxation

You know how you don't miss something until it's gone? Well sometimes you don't realise how tense you are until you relax. This relaxation technique is all about making you aware of how a tense muscle feels in order to relax it. Full relaxation is achieved by progressively tensing and relaxing each set of muscles:

1. Lie down somewhere comfortable where you won't be disturbed

2. Breathe nice and easily until you are ready to begin

3. Start with your feet. Tense your feet muscles, pointing your toes downwards, and holding your breath to maintain the tension. Hold for 5 seconds. Relax and breathe out

4. Repeat the process with your ankles, curling your toes up. Move slowly up your body, tensing and then relaxing each set of muscles

5. Follow this sequence: calves, thighs, buttocks, stomach, chest, hands, arms, shoulders, neck and face

6. Finally tense your whole body, hold your breath for a few moments and then relax and breathe out

Exercise 2: The Fantasy Cigarette Exercise

If you don't feel very confident about performing new breathing techniques then you can get along just as well by mimicking a type of breathing that you've been using for years, the kind you use when smoking a cigarette. Let me explain. When you are "stressed-out" and smoke a cigarette, most of the 'relief' you feel is the result of putting nicotine into your system and so easing withdrawal, but part of the benefit is derived from the effect of taking long, deep inhalations as you drag on the cigarette. When we are stressed our breathing becomes shallow and rapid (in extreme cases this can lead to a fully-fledged panic attack) so we need to slow it down and deepen each inhalation in order to relax.

Find a quiet place (away from spectators if possible!) and pretend you are smoking a cigarette. Take ten long, slow drags on your imaginary cigarette, and slow your breathing right down. Lean back and open up your chest as you inhale to the bottom of your lungs then exhale much as you would if you were smoking. You can even pretend to blow smoke rings if you like, just so long as you don't actually have a cigarette! I can almost guarantee that after completing this exercise, your physical stress levels will have dropped a bit and you will feel better able to get on with the rest of the day in a calmer frame of mind.

Exercise 3: Positive Relaxation Imagery
Children regularly use their imaginations to create a pretend world. Sadly, it's a skill we forget as we get older, but imagining a positive and relaxing scene can be therapeutic, and it's not as difficult as you may think. You can base your scene on a real favourite place if you like, such as a holiday destination or even a warm bubble bath! It can be whatever you like!

1. Make yourself comfortable in a quiet place where you won't be disturbed, dim the lighting if you can

2. Close your eyes and imagine your favourite place, consciously relax your shoulders and breathe deeply

3. Focus on the colours in your relaxing place

4. Now focus on one colour

5. Now focus on the sounds

6. Now focus on any smells and aromas

7. Now imagine touching something

8. Lie quietly and enjoy imagining being in this relaxing place for a while

9. When you are ready, open your eyes in your own time

Keep practising this with the same imagined place and you will soon be able to reach a relaxed state quickly. You can even develop a 'short cut' to your relaxed place. When you are there, press your thumb and forefinger together. This is your trigger and soon, when you press your trigger, you will go straight to your imagined place. Adapted from 'Stress Management: a Quick Guide' by Stephen Palmer and Linda Strickland, Daniels Press: tel: 01582 472788)

You might also consider relaxation tapes and classes (yoga, Tai chi, massage, aromatherapy etc.). Exercise is very good for relieving stress and tension, especially swimming. Here are some excellent tips for tricky or stressful situations that I picked up from a publication produced by an organisation called 'ASH in Wales'. I've added some comments of my own but the list is basically theirs.

TWENTY TOP TIPS FOR COPING WITH STRESS

1. **Work off stress**. Physical activity is a terrific outlet. Don't worry if you don't have access to a gym or a swimming pool when a stressful situation arises, a simple walk in the fresh air or a run around the block will have a dramatic effect on your physical and mental stress levels.

2. **Talk to someone you really trust**. Baring your soul to a sympathetic listener can be a great relief. You can tell them about your cravings, the problems you've

encountered that day or have a good old moan about
how rotten everyone else has been! Voicing these
negative thoughts and emotions will help to get them out
of your system so that you can change your mood for the
better.

3. **Learn to accept what you cannot change**. Although
   simple on the face of it, this is a very good piece of
   advice. We all rant and rave about life's injustices, but if
   there really is no prospect of doing anything about a
   particular problem then it's pointless resenting the fact
   for ever. Accept it and move on.

4. **Avoid self-medication with alcohol, cannabis, too
   much coffee or tranquillisers**. If you feel stressed out
   and miserable then these things are unlikely to solve
   your problems. Alcohol may be OK in moderation in
   controlled circumstances (when there is no tobacco
   around to tempt you) but getting 'leg-less' could undo all
   your hard work! Coffee will have more of an effect on
   you after stopping so don't drink too much or you'll get
   'jittery'. Unless you're on prescribed medication from the
   doctor try not to turn to tranquillisers for help with stress
   or you may end up with even more drug problems to
   contend with!

5. **Get enough sleep and rest to recharge your
   batteries**. Now is not the time to burn the candle at both
   ends. A regular good night's sleep is essential to help you
   cope with the hard work of quitting, especially during
   the first 3 weeks.

6. **Take time out to play**. All work and no play will make
   you feel deprived and resentful after a while. Avoid bad
   moods and depression by setting time aside for activities
   that you really enjoy or try out some new ones. You
   might end up surprising yourself!

7. **Do something for others**. Helping someone else can make you fell good too. You don't have to become Mother Theresa overnight but if you're feeling down, then doing someone else a good turn will give you a sense of satisfaction.

8. **Take one thing at a time**. Learn to schedule your tasks properly so that you don't get overloaded. Imagine that you are someone who works for you – you wouldn't expect an employee to carry out 15 tasks simultaneously so don't expect it of yourself.

9. **Agree with somebody**. Life should not be a constant battleground. Avoid entrenched interpersonal conflicts. Think of your coronary arteries instead!

10. **Manage your time better**. You need a system that works for you, not against you.

11. **Plan ahead by saying 'no' now**. You may prevent too much pressure piling up in the future.

12. **If you are ill, don't try to carry on as if you're not**. This is part of learning to read messages from your mind and body. Soldiering on when you're really not up to it is a false economy as you'll end up in even worse shape and may relapse into the bargain.

13. **Develop a hobby**. Work or family commitments can become an addiction and you need something to counterbalance it. You'll be a nicer person to those around you if you have other strings to your bow.

14. **The answer lies with you**. Only you can change the way you react to stress. Don't sit around waiting for someone to wave a magic wand. Think creatively about how to manage your life better and get on with it!

15. **Eat sensibly**. Often the simplest advice is the best. Putting good quality 'fuel' into your body at reasonably

regular intervals will have a profound effect on your
mood and well-being. It will also help to prevent your
blood sugar from falling too low and could stop you from
relapsing.

16. **Don't put off relaxing**. Use a stress reduction
technique daily. Progressive muscular relaxation and
controlled breathing can be very helpful. Learn to
recognise the signs of physical stress build-up, e.g. tight,
tense muscles around the shoulders and neck, rapid
shallow breathing and a general sense of anxiety.

17. **Don't be afraid to say No!** If you keep accepting all the
work that others pile onto you then you've only yourself
to blame if you get overloaded.

18. **Know when you are tired and do something about
it**. OK, so it may not be possible to slip off for a nap
whenever you want to, but even a 5 minute break can
sometimes make a lot of difference to rising stress levels

19. **Delegate responsibility**. A few minutes spent getting
someone else to help you will be time well spent if it
makes your day less hectic.

20. **Be realistic about achieving perfection**. Don't beat
yourself up over the things you haven't managed to do,
concentrate on giving yourself credit for what you have
achieved. No-one succeeds at everything and trying to be
perfect will only result in disappointment!

STRESS-BUSTING AT WORK

If you've been used to smoking at work or in work-breaks, then
you may worry about coping with your first day back at work
after stopping. There are things you can do to help yourself in
this situation and the following tips may help:

1. **Get rid of any ashtrays etc.** from your work area and ask colleagues not to smoke nearby if possible.

2. **Use NRT** to help you function at work and manage cravings more effectively.

3. **Change your break times** and take a short walk in the fresh air or read a book instead of joining colleagues who smoke.

4. **Tell your colleagues** that you are stopping, so that they won't offer you one without realising.

5. **Get little jobs done quickly.** File stuff away so that your desk is less cluttered. Any unnecessary paperwork should be filed under 'B' for bin!

6. **Make a master list** of jobs that need to be done so as to structure your work effectively.

7. **Take a break** if you feel stressed out. Get up and walk around for a few minutes or do a breathing exercise. You'll be more productive and happier if you tackle the problem straightaway.

8. **Treat yourself** to a reward of some kind at lunch time. Go to a good cafe or restaurant, buy yourself something at the shops or settle down to read a favourite novel in the park.

9. **Ask questions** to make sure you know exactly what work you are supposed to be doing. There's nothing worse than slaving away for ages only to find that you should have been doing something else!

10. **Go home!** If things really get on top of you then tell your boss you don't feel too good and get out. You're unlikely to get the sack provided you don't do it every day, and if it prevents you from cracking up it'll be worth it.

STRESS-BUSTING AT HOME

It's no good working hard to eliminate stress in your workplace and then going home to a high stress zone. You need to rest and relax within your own four walls so take steps to avoid unnecessary friction with the people you live with, whether they be partners, parents or children.

How to ensure that a blazing argument doesn't end up with you lighting up.

Family rows, particularly between couples are one of the main reasons ex-smokers give for starting smoking again. So, if you've stopped smoking and you want to avoid relapsing after a row, consider the following:

1. **Remind yourself** that you don't smoke for some very good reasons and never use an argument as an excuse to start again.

2. **Let your partner speak** uninterrupted for five minutes, they may even have a point or perhaps just run out of things to say!

3. **Try complimenting** your partner a couple of times before mentioning the thing that bugs you; believe me flattery works!

4. **Stay seated** when arguing and try not to raise your voice, even when they refuse to remove their nail clippings from the side of the bath yet accuse you of being a slob!

5. **A short walk** around the block and a few deep breaths will help calm you down and may keep you out of the divorce court!

6. **If your partner has got you really mad** then get the hell out of there! Find somewhere quiet and try a breathing exercise or let off some steam through activity.

STRESS-BUSTING FOR PARENTS

Parents who smoke are always having to find ways of satisfying their need for nicotine whilst also satisfying the demands made by their children (and boy can kids be demanding!). Many try not to smoke in front of their kids because they know it sets a bad example and can damage their health but that means that they often have to delay getting their nicotine 'fix' and so their stress levels rise. If the kids are being awkward or refuse to settle so that mum or dad can slip out for a quick fag break then tempers can boil over which isn't good for anyone. Alternatively you might think 'what the hell' and smoke in front of them anyway but then you'll probably end up worrying that they'll start to smoke because of you etc. etc.

Parents can and do quit

Of course smoking doesn't really help you cope with your kids. In fact it sends precious money up in smoke, and makes you feel guilty for inflicting your smoke on them. But when you're hooked, it often seems doubly difficult to quit because you have the stress of kids to deal with. If all this sounds sadly familiar then take heart: 1000's of parents have stopped smoking so it can be done! In fact most people feel much less stressed within a few weeks of stopping. Not least because all the guilt is gone, and because the money they save can be used to treat themselves to something that really will help with stress, like the occasional babysitter! Don't make the mistake of thinking that smoking is all you've got for yourself and that without it life will be all work and no play. Once you've stopped you'll be happier, healthier and probably closer to your kids who will respect you for stopping in the long run. You'll be able to run around and play with them for longer and stay young at heart yourself.

8 ways to avoid stress with young children

1. Be realistic

You can't achieve as much in a day when you have young children to care for so don't expect too much of yourself. Getting through the day is sometimes achievement enough. Set realistic goals. If you can, arrange some time for yourself. Hand the kids over to a friend or a relative for a while whilst you get on top of a few jobs or take a much-needed break. You could offer to return the favour later (preferably when you're not in the middle of quitting smoking).

2. Keep them busy and active

Bored kids are difficult kids! Try to keep them busy doing something constructive. Sending them up a chimney with a brush isn't recommended these days, but most kids will need plenty of stimulation to keep them interested and positive. Physical activity will help them burn up excess energy, keep them more relaxed and make it easier for them to settle at bedtime.

3. Take time out

Taking a break is very important, but you don't have to smoke to relax. Find something else to do with the time. Drink some orange juice, slap on a 'face pack', phone a friend or watch TV.

4. Keep your cool

Everyone gets angry sometimes, it's natural. But try to learn what it is that your kids do to wind you up the most! Then, when they do it, instead of reacting immediately take a deep breath to calm yourself first. Getting angry and shouting will get your child wound up as well. Be calm, clear and firm. You'll be more effective and less stressed out.

5. The power of planning

Good planning can save you a lot of unnecessary stress. That manic morning rush could be made easier if you spent five minutes the night before organising packed lunches, clothes and shoes to be ready, and when you go to the supermarket remember to write a list first. That way you won't need to worry about what you need while the kids are shouting and it will help you to say no to demands for more chocolate and toys. Some supermarkets (e.g. Safeway) now have excellent crèche facilities for younger children so you can drop them off before you shop and cruise the aisles in peace (bliss!).

6. Establish a regular routine
Children like to know what's coming next! A regular routine in the morning and at bedtime means they'll know what to expect so they'll be less inclined to 'try it on'. An evening ritual of bath and a story before bed may seem to take more time but it helps them settle and it could save you running the equivalent of a marathon up and down the stairs telling them to be quiet!

7. Get them involved
Kids love to have a 'job' to do and to be involved in grown-up activities. For example, when you are in the supermarket why not let them help choose which type of jam to buy or send them off to search for the sausages. It'll take longer this way, but it may prevent the tears and the tantrums.

8. Get a life!
Make time for yourself. Your family are important but you need time for yourself too. Try to schedule in regular activities with friends. A trip to the gym, cinema or a coffee with a mate while someone else takes the kids. Don't put your needs at the bottom of the list or you'll end up feeling bitter and resentful.

9. Enjoy your kids
Try to enjoy your time with your children. They may drive you mad at the moment, but don't forget, kids grow up fast and before you realise it this stage will be over. Who knows, you may even find you miss it!

CHAPTER 11

Special Cases

STOPPING IN PREGNANCY

Every woman who has been pregnant knows how it feels to be treated like a walking womb, when it feels like everyone cares more about the baby than you. But if you are among the one in four pregnant women who smoke regularly, everyone has something to say – and it's rarely good. Pregnant smokers don't need constant criticism – they need information, understanding and support. Most people now accept that smoking during pregnancy can pose a risk to both the mother and the baby but being pregnant won't necessarily make it easy to stop, as I know to my cost.

The thin blue line

When I became pregnant with my first child ten years ago I was thrilled. I'd wanted to have a baby for some years but I'd been told by doctors that it might not be possible for me. The realisation that I really was pregnant was fantastic and I gazed at the little blue line in the pregnancy test window in delight. Things would have to change of course; I knew that and I was well aware that my previous lifestyle of drinking, smoking and partying wasn't exactly ideal for an expectant mum.

Identity crisis

Having your first baby can be a real milestone in your life as it marks the end of your carefree youth and the beginning of a new phase of life that will bring serious responsibilities as you do your best to care for your child. Although I was happy to be pregnant I think I was also frightened that I was about to lose my identity. I saw myself as a rather wild, rebellious young woman with a fondness for staying out late in pubs and at parties. I enjoyed getting drunk, smoking, and going to rock concerts. I knew that I wouldn't be able to carry on doing all of these things but I didn't know who or what I would become when they were no longer possible. I would become a mother of course and look after my baby to the best of my ability but what else would there be? Would I still have a personality after the birth? It might sound strange but I think I was deeply unsure about my changing role and it was frightening to be on the verge of such a huge transition in my way of life.

Sickness didn't stop me

I hoped and naively expected to find that giving up smoking and drinking would be easy because I was pregnant. I'd heard of other women being completely put off by the smell or sight of tobacco and assumed that this would happen to me too. I thought that morning sickness and the physical changes resulting from the pregnancy would magically transform me into some kind of perfect 'earth-mother' type and that the required change of lifestyle would be relatively effortless. I was wrong. Morning sickness came and went during the first three months as expected, but it didn't diminish my craving for nicotine, if anything it made it stronger because I felt lousy and wanted my usual 'comforts' all the more. I'd smoke in between bouts of sickness and the more I tried to stop, the more dispirited I became when each attempt failed.

Shamed in public

I became a secretive smoker as time went by, especially once my pregnancy began to show. I felt the shame of being a pregnant smoker very keenly and avoided smoking in public whenever possible because I didn't want to be judged by strangers. One incident that sticks in my mind happened when I was about 6 months pregnant. I was waiting for my husband at an airport somewhere. I smoked a cigarette as I stood there with the luggage and all of a sudden an American lady came up and shouted at me. She accused me of deliberately harming my unborn baby and told me in no uncertain terms that it was terrible to smoke while pregnant. My eyes filled with tears of shame and embarrassment. I knew she was right and in my heart I agreed with her but at that moment I wanted the floor to open up and swallow me. I remember saying 'Thank you for your advice' and then moving away from her as quickly as possible. It was a real low point but sadly even that didn't make me feel able to stop and I continued to smoke for the rest of the pregnancy despite numerous doomed attempts to quit.

My dirty secret

At the beginning of my pregnancy the midwife and the doctor had enquired about my smoking habits and I assured them first that I was cutting right down and then that I had stopped. It was true that I'd tried to cut down, but I never managed to stop completely. I was just saying what they wanted to hear so that they wouldn't probe too closely or read me the riot act. At that time I knew very little about what it takes to stop successfully. I think if someone had given me practical advice on stopping and had sympathised with my sense of shame, I might have been able to succeed but as it was it remained my 'dirty secret' until after delivery when, like so many other mums, I started to smoke openly again.

Success at last

Luckily I did manage to stop a few years later but, as a result of my experiences, I identify strongly with pregnant smokers who find it tough to quit. It's crucial that they receive maximum support to stop and that they don't get treated as second class citizens by health professionals.

It's never too late

On a more positive note, pregnant women can pack up at any stage during their pregnancy and still feel the benefit. Let's take a look at the facts:

Planning a baby?

If you smoke and are planning a baby, you may take longer to conceive and suffer other problems. The extent of reduced fertility depends on how much you smoke. The risk of having an ectopic pregnancy (where the egg establishes itself outside the uterus) is doubled, and the chance of a miscarriage increased by 27%: if you can manage to stop smoking prior to conception then the chances are you will return to a normal level of fertility and significantly reduce other risks.

Stopping while pregnant

Smoking during pregnancy increases the likelihood of vomiting, urinary infections, thrush and feeling unwell during your pregnancy, but once you stop, you'll feel better even allowing for the nicotine withdrawal process.

Smoking and birthweight

Women who smoke during pregnancy are three times more likely to have a low birth-weight baby and this is strongly associated with the risk of death and serious illness in your infant. Some women resist this idea and the decrease in birthweight for each individual baby may be pretty small, but it is significant at this vital stage in a child's development. Still births and early deaths are increased by approximately a third in babies of smokers. If you can stop smoking in the first three months of pregnancy then the impact of your smoking on the weight of your baby will be reduced, so don't think that after the first few weeks the damage is done.

Cutting down

Unfortunately, cutting down on smoking during pregnancy doesn't reduce the risks to your baby and, as I explained earlier in the book, it's seldom an effective way of stopping completely. Pregnant women may often tell their doctors/midwives that they've cut down to appease them (as I did) but in reality many of them are probably smoking just as much as before, or extracting more from the few cigarettes they do have.

Stopping smoking *at any time* will benefit your baby. Smoking in late pregnancy is related to wheezing and breathlessness – it's never too late to stop!

Partner problems

Sadly it seems that men are often less than helpful when their partners become pregnant. More than four out of five pregnant smokers have a partner who smokes, and nearly two thirds of these guys have suggested their partners quit. But only 6% actually give up themselves, and just 27% cut down or smoke away from their partners. If your partner recognises the need to make your home a healthier place for a baby on the way then try to persuade him to give up with you, it will improve your chances of success and will be of enormous benefit to his health as well as the baby's. Don't be too forceful, though, if he really isn't ready then too much pressure could be counter-productive.

STOPPING WITH ASTHMA

Although it seems like common sense to say that smoking is bad for asthmatics and will make their condition worse over time (as indeed it will), the reality may *feel* very different for the asthmatic who is also a smoker. If you are suffering from an asthma attack or are having some breathing problems then the situation is often made worse by stress and anxiety. Asthmatics who are also smokers often find that when they light up a cigarette their breathing actually improves as their bronchial system relaxes and their stress levels fall due to the relief of their nicotine withdrawal systems. This being the case, although they know that smoking is bad for them, they fear that stopping smoking may make matters worse.

Visit your doctor before you stop

If you suffer from asthma and you are also considering stopping smoking then pay a visit to your doctor before your Quit Day and tell him/her what you are going to do. Your asthma may get worse for a few weeks after stopping, so it's a good idea to have your medication adjusted to cope with this transition period. In the slightly longer term there may well be a drastic improvement in your condition, so you have everything to gain by quitting. I've seen asthmatics, who were on a whole range of treatments before stopping, improve to such a degree that they can manage with the barest minimum afterwards, and the quality of their lives has improved dramatically as a result.

Last Words

If after reading this book you feel ready to have a go at stopping, or have already done so then you have all my good luck wishes. Try not to worry about the possibility of failure – all of us make mistakes from time to time, but it's our reaction to setbacks that make all the difference. If you accept past mistakes as 'water under the bridge' and move forward positively then your changes of long-term success will be greater than before. Analyse why previous relapses have occurred and plan to avoid similar situations in the future.

There is no shame in trying and failing, as any effort that goes into stopping smoking is never wasted. The worst situation would be not trying at all because of fear of failure. When, as children, we first learn to walk there is a great deal of stumbling and tottering involved before we finally learn to cope on two feet. It is our persistence and our ability to learn from experience that eventually win the day and so it is with stopping smoking. Some people manage to put all the pieces of the stopping 'puzzle' together earlier than others but for most people a degree of trial and error is likely before the reward of success is earned.

Once you have managed to escape from the tobacco trap, it's important to maintain a tolerant attitude towards those around you who still smoke. Their problem was your problem and whilst you have every right to shield yourself from the effects of their smoke, it is only fair to respect their decision to carry on smoking for the time being. Your success may at first make them feel defensive, as it begs the question as to why they are still smoking, but in time your achievement may inspire them to have a go too. Nagging your loved ones about their smoking can make matters worse but your silent success can speak volumes.

Good luck.
Nicola Willis

Where to Get Help & Information

GET ON THE NET!

These days, as more and more people are installing computers at low cost, it's getting ever easier to access the Internet and to discover, from the comfort of your own home (or someone else's), how much is going on out in the big wide world of stopping smoking. There's a mass of fascinating and useful information on all aspects of tobacco on the 'Master Tobacco Page' at: **www.tobacco.org**, from where you can explore many tobacco-related sites according to your interests – news, history, medical research etc.

Get on-line for an easier time

If you're a would-be stopper, the chances are that you'll be feeling somewhat isolated and could use all the help and encouragement you can get. So why not find some on-line support and advice at **www.quitsmokingsupport.com** ? This friendly and popular interactive website originates from the US. The hosts claim to have had over 1.3 million visitors in the last year (or 4 per minute) and the site provides free resources aiming to 'assist smokers in their desire to quit'.

Just Browsing

As well as linking to another 60 of the best quitting sites, and offering free subscription to a discussion group and newsletter, the **'quit smoking support'** site offers an 'interactive area'. Here the pages include a book-store, a guest book, an ex-smokers' list (feel free to add your name). You can find information on teen-smoking, read inspirational letters and comments, and there's a substantial page dedicated to post-quitting weight-gain with lots of lip-smacking, low-calorie recipes and exercise advice.

Chatterbox?

When it comes to 'chatting', you can browse through the 'Bulletin Board', the 'Chat Room' or ' The Basement'. The 'Bulletin Board' is an excellent support area, dealing with any topic related to quitting and there are hundreds of messages for you to browse through. After reading this book you may be able to answer someone else's questions or offer support to a fellow quitter anywhere in the world. The problems people face and the feelings they experience when quitting smoking are pretty universal so you may find that you have heaps in common with stoppers from Minneapolis to Moscow!

Here are some examples of messages posted on the bulletin board:

'Worried about Sally – lost contact – how's it going?'

'It's been 6 weeks, 3 days and I've not smoked 1000 sickarettes! Yippee!'

'Made it to 5 days ... barely!'

'I'm expecting a baby, should I use patches?'

'What is Zyban and where can I get it?'

Buddy-up!

Contributors to the 'Bulletin Board' page often relate their own quitting experiences, maybe giving tips for success, or asking for advice; others respond with congratulations or words of encouragement and, of course, you can join in too! Get acquainted with a few new 'buddies', follow each other's progress or get help to deal with relapse. You'll find it raises your morale no end. And if you get sick of talking about (not) smoking, get some relief in 'The Basement', an area for general, *non*-smoking-related chat!

24-hour support

Smoking cessation support never sleeps on the net. When you get a craving in the middle of the night or when you're feeling lonely and on the verge of relapse, try logging on: you could get an enormous boost from contact with others who know what you're going through and who will urge you towards success.

Got the history bug?

If, like me, you find the history of tobacco use utterly fascinating (yes, I am a tobacco anorak!), you may like to know that there are pages and pages of historical material about tobacco and smoking at **www.tobacco.org** on the **'History'** and **'Tobacco Timeline'** sites. With a little exploration, you can discover more about smoking through the ages. You could find out how Native Americans used to give themselves tobacco enemas for psychedelic purposes(!) or, if that's not to your taste you could delve into the tales of the early buccaneers and adventurers who first encountered the strange practice of smoking in the New World. There are facts and figures about the massive quantities of cigarettes that have been sold this century, along with the comparably huge revenues successive governments have extracted in tobacco duties. You can find out about the history of cigarette advertising and learn more about the rivalry between major tobacco companies.

RELATED RESOURCES
FOR HEALTH PROFESSIONALS

If it's part of your job to help people stop smoking, or you want to know more about organisations that specialise in this subject, then the following information may be useful:

Action on Smoking & Health (ASH)

ASH have associate offices around the world and are an excellent source of information on all aspects of smoking cessation and tobacco control. The London branch publishes a useful bi-monthly journal called 'Burning Views' and they can be reached on **0270 739 5902**

Quit/Quitline (UK Smoking Cessation Charity)

Quit provide a telephone counselling line for stoppers in need of counselling and advice on the best ways to stop. Their staff are highly trained and the organisation also produces a useful range of leaflets and resources on different aspects of quitting, e.g. weight-gain and stopping in pregnancy. If you are a health professional who can offer services to local quitters then Quit may be able to refer callers who live in your area to the services you provide. Quit also run an annual award scheme for successful quitters called 'The Quitter of the Year Award'. To contact Quit call: **0270 388 5775** or ring the Quitline on **0800 00 22 00.**

STOP! Magazine Ltd

STOP! Magazine is a monthly, self-help magazine for people who want to stop smoking. It is available on subscription and also from newsagents, supermarkets and pharmacies in the UK. It combines the motivational success stories of celebrities and ordinary stoppers who have beaten the weed, with up-to-date information about treatments and services. Each edition also features articles on issues of interest to quitters, e.g. relapse, weight-gain, health and teen-smoking. The advice and information presented is research-based and ethical. A must for every doctor's waiting–room! At the time of writing a US version of the magazine is in development. You can contact the STOP! Magazine team at 70C, High Street, Whitstable, Kent, CT5 1DP. **Tel: 01227 779229 Fax: 01227 779228** or visit the website at **www.stopmagazine.co.uk**

Carbon Monoxide Monitors

If you run a service for smokers then you really should get hold of a Carbon Monoxide Monitor so that you can check the readings of your patients/clients before and after they stop. You can obtain monitors from either of the following companies:

Bedfont Ltd
Bedfont House, Holywell Lane, Sittingbourne,
Kent, ME9 7HN. Tel: **01634 375 164**

Micro Medical
PO Box 6, Rochester, Kent, ME1 2AZ. Tel: **01703 663976**

Monographs on smoking

Report of the US Surgeon General (1988) *The health conse-quences of smoking: Nicotine addiction*. US DHSS, Rockville, MD. (This weighty tome is a bit academic and may seem slightly out of date but it is still full of useful information and its publication was a landmark event in the history of tobacco control.)

Wonnacott, S., Russell, M. & Stolerman, I. (1990) *Nicotine psy-chopharmacology: molecular, cellular and behavioural aspects*. Oxford: Oxford University Press. (Comprehensive and academic, not for beginners!)

West, R. & Gossop, M. (1994) *Comparing drugs of dependence*. Addiction, 89, Number 11. A special issue of the journal on comparing drugs of dependence. (An expert review of all aspects of smoking and nicotine addiction.)

Journals

Tobacco Control is the premier journal on tobacco policy issues. It comes out quarterly and orders should be sent to: BMJ Publishing Group, PO Box 299, London, WC1H 9TD

Nicotine & Tobacco Research has just been launched and covers studies ranging from molecular biology to epidemiology. You can get subscribption information on **http://www.srnt.org**

Addiction is the best among many other journals reporting studies of smoking. It is published monthly and also covers the full range of addictive drugs and behaviours in modern society. Orders should be directed to: Carfax Publishing, Customer Services, Rankine Road, Basingstoke, RG24 8PR.

Key smoking studies tend also to be published in the main medical journals such as; The New England Journal of Medicine, JAMA, The Lancet, The BMJ and The Archives of Internal Medicine (all of which can be found in medical libraries).

Abstracts of current literature on smoking

Medline Updates 23: Smoking: this is a monthly service and is available from the British Library. Call 0270 4127469 for more information.

Addiction Abstracts: A quarterly journal containing information on studies relating to addiction (call 01235 521154 for information); http://www.ahcpr.gov/guide/ A comprehensive resource for anyone interested in smoking.

The Cochrane Library: Includes meta-analyses and reviews of studies of smoking cessation methodology. Distributed on CD-ROMS, many medical libraries have it. Get more information on: http://www/cochrane.co.uk. Relevant abstracts are on: http://hiru.mcmaster.ca/cochrane/cochrane/revabstr/g16index.htm

Internet discussion forums

Globalink – An internet discussion forum covering a wide range of smoking topics and news. To register, e-mail them on globalink@globalink.org

The Society for Research on Nicotine and Tobacco (SRNT) provides an internet discussion forum with a focus on US issues. It is open to people who have published research papers on smoking. For information, e-mail genin@srnt.org or go to http://www.srnt.org

To apply to join a *UK smoking cessation discussion forum*, e-mail Smoking-cessation-request@mailbase.ac.uk

Index